CHILDREN'S
WELFARE &
CHILDREN'S
RIGHTS

A PRACTICAL GUIDE TO THE LAW

Wendy Stainton Rogers
& Jeremy Roche

Hodder & Stoughton

A MEMBER OF THE HODDER HEADLINE GROUP

We dedicate this book to our children Amanda, Arjun, Karina and Rebekah.

Cataloguing in Publication Data is available from the British Library

ISBN 0 340 58512 9

First published 1994
Impression number 10 9 8 7 6 5 4 3 2 1
Year   1998 1997 1996 1995 1994

Copyright © 1994 Wendy Stainton Rogers and Jeremy Roche

Typeset by Wearset, Boldon, Tyne and Wear
Printed in Great Britain for Hodder & Stoughton Educational, a division of Hodder Headline Plc, 338 Euston Road, London NW1 3BH by Page Bros (Norwich) Ltd.

Contents

FIGURES

BOXES

COURT ORDER BOXES

Acknowledgements

We suspect that writing this book has been harder on our partners than on us – they too have their own books to write, jobs to do and battles to fight, and we have often been preoccupied when they have needed us. We are grateful to Shirin Rai and Rex Stainton Rogers for their forbearance and support. We also gratefully acknowledge Rae Smyth for all the help and support she has given us. We thank Amanda Leak, Sue Shephard, Rupert Hughes, Eleri Rees, Leonie Jordan, Tina Herring and Nick Allen for commenting on the final draft, although, of course, all the errors are ours alone.

We gratefully acknowledge the Open University for giving us permission to reproduce Figures 2.1, 3.1 and 5.1 and Peter Greenland for permission to reproduce the cover photograph.

Finally we would like to thank each other – for being such a good person with whom to work, and for each other's friendship. It has not only survived the task of writing this book, but been strengthened by it.

1 Introduction

When we think about the law, the images most readily brought to mind are often those of law courts, witness boxes and bewigged judges. But, in fact, the law is woven much more into our daily lives than that. Our working environments are regulated by legislation over health and safety, our homes by building regulations, our shopping by laws of contract and consumer protection, and so on. Indeed, there is almost no area of our lives that is untouched by law.

When we come to consider the law in relation to children's rights and welfare, then this is just as true. While it may be court battles over taking children into care or between divorcing parents which hit the headlines, in actual fact these are pretty rare occurrences when compared with the more everyday impact of the law. This is true both of what is sometimes called 'private law' (that concerning family relationships between parents and their children) and 'public law' (that involving the state, to do with things like the provision of services for children and child protection).

The law, for instance, legislates over what it means to be a 'parent' and 'a child', the limits of parental authority, and when and under what circumstances children can make decisions for themselves. It specifies that local authorities have certain obligations towards children, ranging from a duty to safeguard their welfare and investigate referrals of possible abuse, to being obliged to provide family centres. Those who offer services to children (such as day care) are regulated by legislation which specifies things like floor area, staffing and the number of lavatories.

A great deal of this legislation is only observable to most people in its effects (such as being told who is the 'designated' teacher in a school, the person who deals with allegations of abuse). It is often hard to see where it is coming from or how it is put into practice. We will begin this chapter, therefore, with a brief description of how the law gets made and how it gets filtered down to those who must enact it.

In this book, our aim will be to provide a practical, user-friendly guide to the current law in England and Wales as it applies to considerations of children's welfare. Most critically, we will be concerned with the legal framework introduced in 1989 by the Children Act – a far-reaching and comprehensive piece of legislation which has brought about, since its full implementation in 1991, very considerable changes in the way that children's welfare is tackled. It covers 'private' areas, such as parenthood and arrangements made following parental separation, and 'public' areas of law, including services provided for children and their families, child protection and care and supervision.

However, this is not 'just another book on the Children Act'. We have also addressed a range of other legislation which impacts upon children's welfare, including, for example, those aspects of the 1991 Criminal Justice Act dealing with child witnesses, the law in relation to child abduction, and those provisions of criminal law which place children and young people in local authority accommodation. In other words, what we have tried to do is to work from the situations in which professionals and volunteers who work with children find themselves, and examine how these are affected by the law.

What is in the book?

We begin the book with the legal system itself. Chapter 2 outlines things like the way law is made, changed and disseminated (via, for example, Government Guidance documents). It also sets out some of the basic features of the Children Act. Chapter 3 looks specifically at the notion of parenthood and at what happens when there are disputes about arrangements for children's upbringing. Chapter 4 examines the provision of welfare services for children and their families, and chapter 5 focuses on child protection.

These chapters cover information which is relevant to all those whose work or responsibilities bring them into contact with children and young people. We next move on to consider two areas in more detail – the education service in chapter 6 and the health service in chapter 7. While these also contain material of general interest, their primary purpose is to set out how child welfare law relates to working in these two fields.

Chapter 8 is about statutory intervention in children's lives – care and supervision proceedings. Chapter 9 covers children and young people living away from home, including not only those who are 'in care' but also young offenders, children living in hospitals and nursing homes, and those who are in boarding schools of various kinds.

Our final chapter focuses, particularly, on issues of children's rights. We review in what ways the law can be seen as 'good for children', and how it may be used not only to promote and safeguard their welfare, but also to foster and promote their rights.

Special Features

Above all, we wanted the book to be useful – not a dry tome, but something which will really help you get on top of what is, to be fair, a very extensive and complex body of legislation. We have done this in two ways.

First, you will see that the text is broken up by a number of devices. These include short 'case studies' which illustrate how various bits of the law may work in practice; 'boxes' which summarise critical points; and 'Court Order boxes' which provide systematic information about the various orders that courts can make. These will offer you useful forms of reference and a quick and easy way of finding which part of the Act you may need to consult.

Second, you will find at the end of the book some additional sections intended to help you get to grips with the law. We have included a detailed glossary which defines a large number of legal and other terms which are used in relation to welfare provision, services and processes of law, etc. We also provide a comprehensive list of suggestions about further reading, and some useful addresses of organisations which you may want to consult and which offer advice and information.

PRINCIPLES AND PURPOSES OF CHILD WELFARE LAW

In this chapter we will begin our examination of child welfare law by picking up some of its features, the principles on which it is based and what, in particular, the Children Act 1989 is seeking to achieve

A new concept of parenthood

The Children Act introduces the term *parental responsibility*, which is defined as 'all the rights, duties, powers, responsibilities and authority which by law a parent of a child has in relation to the child and his property' [s3(1)]. Although this definition is not all that different from the idea of 'parental rights' which went before, the Act makes three fundamental changes in how this parental responsibility works.

1   It provides relatively simple ways for people other than a child's 'natural', married parents to acquire parental responsibility.
2   It makes parental responsibility an *enduring commitment*, encouraging parents to continue to be involved in their children's lives and upbringing even if the child ceases to live with them.
3   It allows for parental responsibility to be shared – between parents following divorce, for example, or between a child's birth parent(s) and foster-parents.

In making these innovations, the Children Act is responding to social changes which have led to a high proportion of children these days being born to co-habiting parents, being brought up in re-ordered families (i.e. with step-parents) or by other relatives (e.g. grandparents). The aim is to accommodate these social changes in ways which strengthen rather than weaken family ties.

– BRENDAN'S STORY –

Brendan's parents, Tom and Maggie, have never married, but Tom came to a formal agreement with Maggie so that he acquired parental responsibility for his son soon after Brendan was born. Thus, during the time Tom and Maggie lived together, both of them had an equal role, in law, in Brendan's upbringing. This continued even when Maggie left Tom and went to live with Bill, taking Brendan with her.

At the age of six, when Brendan had been living with Maggie and Bill for two years, they applied to the court for a Residence Order. Tom was consulted and he agreed not to contest the application. A Residence Order was made, giving Bill parental responsibility for Brendan and specifying that Brendan would live with Bill and Maggie. Contact between Brendan and his father, Tom, was agreed between them amicably.

At this point, Maggie, Tom and Bill all had parental responsibility for Brendan. This meant that, for example, any one of them could agree to Brendan receiving medical treatment, and all three were entitled to receive school reports and stand for election as parent governors at Brendan's school.

Tom continued to have Brendan to stay every other weekend and for some parts of school holidays. In virtually all respects, even though Brendan did not live with him, he continued to be able to act as Brendan's parent, though (because of the Residence Order) he could not just decide to have Brendan come and live with him.

As can be seen from Brendan's story, the Act introduced new ways for resolving disputes about children's upbringing, replacing the awarding of 'custody' and 'care and control' with specific orders dealing with things like where a child will live and arrangements for contact between a child and parent. As well as being used when parents separate, these 'section 8 orders' (which are described in detail in chapter 3) offer a highly flexible set of options which can be used for a much wider range of purposes. The orders are focused in their effect. They are intended to resolve just those specific issues which are in dispute (indeed, one is called a Specific Issues Order), rather than undermining the fundamental parent–child relationship.

Knowledge of the legal basis and consequences of parenthood is important. For example, when the parents' relationship breaks down, this can have far-reaching consequences for the children involved. Anybody engaged with looking after those children needs to know where they stand on issues like who has the authority to take them away on holiday, make decisions about their education, consent to their medical treatment and so on. In our example, Brendan's teachers, his doctor and even people like his scoutmaster need to know that Tom, Bill and Maggie all have parental responsibility and that all of them, therefore, have the authority to give permission for Brendan to go away on a trip or be medically examined. They also need to know about the Residence Order and its implications.

Welfare Services

The Children Act specifies that services provided for children and their families must be based on five important, interlinked principles:

1 While services can be provided for all children, local authorities have a statutory duty to provide a range of services for children who are 'in need', in order to promote the ability of their parents to look after them.

2 Services must be offered and delivered on the basis of *partnership* with parents – as a genuine service to families, not a form of covert intervention imposed upon families.

3 Services that are provided must, in particular, address children's needs in terms of their race, culture, religion and language.

4 The different agencies involved in providing services must collaborate together to offer families co-ordinated support.

5 The range and level of services provided must be tailored to identified needs, rather than families having to take pot luck

from those available. Service provision must therefore be strategically planned.

The intention is that welfare provision should be positive – to help families cope with difficulties so that they can care for their children themselves, and to promote children's welfare and healthy development. Not surprisingly, there have been accusations that this shift is largely illusory – it sounds good in theory, but it is extremely difficult (if not impossible) to put into practice without sufficient resources. Moreover, there are some who regard it as hypocritical in that, for all its apparent user-friendliness, there will always be a level of implicit compulsion. It has been argued that families in trouble will be made offers they cannot, in effect, refuse – if they do not accept the 'help' proffered, then this will be taken as evidence that enforced intervention is justified. Critics have argued that, for all the rhetoric about making services for socially and economically disadvantaged families more like the ones that better-off parents arrange and pay for themselves, this is just not achievable in practice.

The response of those who drafted and promoted the Act is that, despite all the practical problems, significant improvements can be achieved by a change in ethos. If local authority staff see themselves as assisting families to care for their children, then the sense of stigma attached to welfare provision can be gradually overcome. Once this happens, they argue, families will become more willing to seek help early on, before situations get too serious – the need for enforced intervention will be genuinely reduced.

To be fair, it is extremely difficult for legislation to engender this kind of change in ethos, especially during recessionary times. Certainly, changing the law, on its own, cannot guarantee that things will be done differently or that public perception will undergo any dramatic turnabout. Nevertheless, the sheer scope of the legislative change within the Children Act and the impact of its range of new provisions do offer, at least, a framework for making the move towards a more positive system of welfare service delivery. It seeks to achieve this in a number of ways.

Targeting services for children in need

Given the severe resource constraints under which local authorities have to operate, the Act adopts a policy of targeting welfare services on those children and families most in need of them. It introduces the concept of *children in need* (which includes disabled children) and sets out, in considerable detail, the kinds of services which must be provided for them. (These are detailed in chapter 4).

Working in partnership with parents

Among all the debate surrounding the Children Act 1989, one issue did command wide agreement – that the success of the Act would, in large measure, depend on the willingness and ability of local authorities to provide the right kinds of assistance to families at the right time. Local authorities are therefore required to develop ways of working with families and children which actively promote their participation, offer them real choices, and genuinely involve them in the decisions affecting them. For example, local authorities are expected to develop procedures for involving parents in case conferences as the norm rather than the exception. Parents should be offered support to help them do this in a positive manner – not just sitting on the sidelines, but contributing information and taking part in decision-making.

Wherever possible, help should be offered on a voluntary basis. For example, the Act directs that local authorities must be willing to provide children with accommodation in the form of a short-term foster placement on an entirely voluntary basis. In such circumstances, parents are free to take their children back home without having to seek permission or give notice. This undoubtedly poses problems for social services, but such arrangements were considered crucial if this was to be seen as a service rather than enforced intervention.

Care consistent with race, culture, religion and language

The Act specifically requires that children should receive care consistent with their racial, cultural, religious and linguistic background. Schedule 2 makes this quite explicit in terms of day care and the recruitment of foster carers. More generally, in terms of good practice, there is a recognition that caring for children and young people involves promoting their self-respect and pride in their cultural identity. Services provided for children and their families should not only be based on anti-discriminatory practice (i.e. practice which challenges racism and other forms of prejudice), but must also offer positive experiences which foster the values and lifestyle of their cultural heritage. In other words, it is not enough to make sure that the staff who work in a particular nursery are not racist or religiously bigoted. Where children who attend the nursery come from different ethnic or racial groups, then things like the food served, religious holidays observed and the children's toys should reflect this ethnic diversity.

Co-ordinating service provision

The Act requires local authorities to co-operate with other agencies and empowers them to request the help of other authorities in the discharge of their duties. Those authorities so requested are under a duty to 'comply with the request if it is compatible with their own statutory duty and does not unduly prejudice the discharge of any of their functions' [s27(1) & (2)]. This includes other local authorities, education, housing and health authorities or NHS trusts, and 'any person authorised by the Secretary of State for the purposes of this section' (e.g. the NSPCC).

This co-operative framework is not intended to result in various authorities passing the buck. For example, the *Code of Guidance for Local Authorities on Homelessness* (1991) refers to the right of the local authorities to request help from any local housing authority and states:

> *The Secretaries of State are concerned to avoid any possibility that the implementation of the 1989 Act might result in children and young people being sent to and fro between departments or authorities.*
> [para 6.16]

The emphasis is on the setting up of appropriate organisational links to ensure collaboration and co-operation. The idea is that, when a family faces difficulties in caring for their children, they should not be passed from one agency to another, trying to get the help that they need. Instead, they should be offered co-ordinated support which brings together, via a simple system they can understand, the necessary mix of services they require to help them out of their difficulties.

– KELLY AND MARTIN'S STORY –

Kelly is four and Martin is eighteen months old. Their father, Mike, was made redundant a year ago and, just recently, the mortgage on the family home was foreclosed and the family made homeless.

For six weeks now they have been living in a one-bedroom flat on the tenth floor of a dilapidated tower block. The flat is cramped and damp, with mould growing on the walls. The kitchen is infested with cockroaches and the electricity supply has been cut off for non-payment.

Their mother, Kaye, is suffering with severe depression, and she and Mike have been having serious arguments. Mike has moved out to live with his brother. Kaye is finding it impossible to cope with the two children on her own. She asks for help from her health visitor. She is especially worried as Martin has become very sickly. She finds it very difficult to leave the flat to go shopping as the lift often does not work.

The health visitor contacts social services. Martin and Kelly are identified as children in need. This places the local authority under an obligation to arrange welfare services for the family. The kinds of things this may include are rehousing, marriage counselling for Kaye and Mike, a nursery place for Kelly and day care for Martin. They should also receive advice on benefits and getting the electricity reconnected. The social worker will therefore have to co-ordinate her work with the benefits office, housing department, voluntary agencies and the education department.

The legislation does not, of course, offer a magic wand which can summon up, for example, appropriate housing out of thin air. As experience with the 1981 Education Act has shown, even where a legal obligation exists (in this case, to provide education services for a child with designated special educational needs), it can be a frustrating and time-consuming business to enforce such an obligation (for example, by way of judicial review, see chapter 2).

Nevertheless, certainly in principle, the intention is that it is not only better but ultimately also more economic to rehouse a family than provide accommodation for children (for example, in foster care). The Act also provides social services departments with a lever to get other departments to co-operate more than they have done in the past.

Strategic planning

In the past, it was felt that families often faced a situation where the services on offer did not really meet their needs. They had to take pot luck from what was available – where there were gaps in provision, there was nothing that could be done. The Children Act seeks to turn this situation around by specifying a new approach to the planning and delivery of services.

Local authorities are required to identify all the children in need in their locality and are empowered to conduct an assessment of these needs. This should identify each child's (and their family's) needs for specific services. However, the purpose of this exercise is not just to make sure individual children and families get the services they need. It also has a critical role to play in strategic planning. Local authorities are expected to gather together the information necessary to plan (in conjunction with other agencies, including health authorities, voluntary organisations and self-help groups, etc.) a comprehensive, integrated, effective system of service provision and delivery. The idea is that, by such an exercise (in conjunction with an audit of existing services), duplication and inefficiency can be resolved, gaps identified and provided for, and systems set up to make services needs-led rather than bureaucracy dominated.

Child protection

The Children Act legislation was drafted and debated in Parliament against a backcloth of concern about child abuse, particularly a growing concern about the sexual abuse of children. The previous law was seen as failing to provide a coherent framework for responding to the different ways in which children may be mistreated. It was also seen as leading to practice which, at times, was itself abusive. The Children Act provided an opportunity for a complete overhaul in the protection of children from abuse.

Its cornerstone principle is that, all other things being equal, children do better when they are brought up and cared for within their families. Within this perspective, the only justification for enforced intervention is when this is necessary to protect the child. This principle was expressly stated by the Lord Chancellor:

> *It is important for the law in a free society expressly to protect the integrity and independence of families, save when there is the least likelihood of significant harm to the child within the family.*
> (Hansard, House of Lords, Second Reading, 6th December, 1988).

The whole thrust of the legislation is to avoid the need to remove children from their families. This is to be achieved in two ways:

1   by providing services to alleviate stresses and to support families coping with difficult times and demanding children (as described in chapter 4) – to avoid situations where the child is exposed to harm in the first place [s17(1)];
2   where the child is at risk of harm, by trying, wherever possible, to reach voluntary agreements with parents about ways of making sure their children are kept safe.

The most favoured option is *prevention*. Where this fails, the next most desirable strategy is intervention on a voluntary basis, in co-operation with the family. In some cases this means, in practice, working with the non-abusing parent. The Act offers some measures to support this. For example, local authorities are given powers to pay for accommodation to allow the person suspected of putting the child at risk to leave the household [Sched 2, para 5]. Only where neither of these options prove practicable is compulsory intervention seen as justified.

The basis for all forms of compulsory intervention is the notion of *significant harm*, and harm is defined as 'ill-treatment or the impairment of health or development', which includes sexual abuse and forms of ill-treatment which are not physical (for more detailed information see chapter 8). This is the critical criterion for deciding whether or not compulsory intervention can be sanctioned.

The Act provides three new orders to enable welfare professionals to take action to protect children – the Child Assessment Order, Emergency Protection Order and Recovery Order. It also clarifies and strengthens police powers to intervene when a child is in immediate danger. New Guidance has been provided in order to improve inter-agency work and to provide an effective infrastructure, at local level, for co-ordinating child protection work. At the same time there have been major improvements in the way that children's testimony may be given in court, in both civil and criminal proceedings. We examine these in detail in chapter 5.

State intervention in children's lives

In the immediate post-war years, the provision of state care for children continued to be overshadowed by the historical legacy of Poor Law legislation. This had been designed to discourage 'parental fecklessness' by placing children in institutions, rather than providing parents with adequate resources to enable them to look after their children themselves. It also reflected the Victorian notion of 'child saving', which had been promoted quite openly by philanthropists like Barnardo in the last century. This was a form of 'social engineering' which sought to rescue children from the damaging influence of negligent and immoral parents and lawless communities. By giving children a 'better' upbringing, such children were to be 'saved' from lives of delinquency and social deviance, and turned into law-abiding, productive citizens.

The introduction of state welfare provisions (such as health care, family allowance and unemployment benefit) undoubtedly enabled far more parents to look after their children themselves. Nevertheless, there continued to be a stigmatisation of some parents as 'inadequate' and, hence, incapable of caring for their children. For example, Jones *et al* (1982) described such parents like this:

> *They tend to come from severely deprived backgrounds, with neurotic and behaviour problems in childhood and adolescence, and frequently delinquency as well. There is often evidence of recurrent mild depressive illness or anxiety states. They are socially isolated and have impaired relationships with families, short courtships, and high levels of marital discord. They are often very young when they marry and pregnancies tend to follow rapidly. Their lifestyle is chaotic with a wide range of social and financial problems. . . . They are unable to cope with ordinary stresses and strains of life.*
>
> (Jones *et al*, 1982, p. 89).

The consequence was that large numbers of children and young people continued to be placed in residential care, in the belief that this was 'saving them' from parents who could not bring them up properly. In practice, this often meant that not only were children removed from their families, but parents were deliberately kept at arms length – allowed little or no contact with their children and assumed incapable of playing any significant role in their children's lives or upbringing.

Over the period from the 1950s up until the 1980s, there was a growing recognition that institutionalisation can be damaging to children, informed particularly by the work of John Bowlby. This led to a shift away from institutional care to foster care. For instance, while in the 1970s it was still common for very young children to be placed in residential nurseries, by the 1980s these establishments were shut down and under-sevens were virtually always placed with foster-parents. By the late 1980s, a number of local authorities had closed down all of their residential establishments and only offered foster care.

Undoubtedly, children were indeed 'rescued' by people like Barnardo from lives of abject poverty, ill-health and danger. That his organisation was also responsible for shipping (often illegally) an estimated 150,000 British children to its colonies between 1618 and 1967 is, perhaps, another matter! Nonetheless, for their day, orphanages, reformatories and 'cottage homes' usually offered children considerably better living conditions and life opportunities than they would have had if they had remained with their parents, at a time when there was no effective system of state benefits.

Sadly, the same cannot be argued today. By the 1980s it was becoming clear that the care system was seriously failing many of the children being drawn into it. It is impossible to know what their lives would have been if they had stayed with their families rather than being taken into 'care', but for many of them it was a severe case of being tipped from the frying-pan into the fire. Stigmatised by the very fact of being 'in care' and frequently experiencing many foster placements which did not work (and hence repeated breakdowns in relationships with their substitute carers), they were often extremely unhappy. Many were entirely unprepared for an independent life once they left care and far too many have today ended up in prisons, living rough on the streets, or simply cut adrift and finding it extremely difficult to cope.

It is not surprising then that there were strong arguments for change. For a start, it was felt that too many children were being needlessly taken into care when, with the right kind of support, they could have stayed at home – hence the kinds of welfare provisions in the Act described in chapter 4. Secondly, too many children were drifting into care following what had originally been intended as only a short-term measure – hence the Act's specification of accommodation as a *service* (also described in chapter 4) which could not be turned into care merely by an administrative ruling. Finally, there was a determination to significantly improve things for those children who do get into the 'care system'.

Changes in the basis of state intervention

The Children Act 1989 radically alters the power of the state to intervene in children's upbringing. Now there is only one avenue by which a local authority can acquire the authority to enforce supervision or undertake long-term parental responsibility for a child – by way of the court making a Supervision Order or a Care Order. For these orders to be made, the court must be satisfied that strictly defined conditions are fulfilled:

1 The child is likely to otherwise suffer significant harm.
2 Failures in the parents' care of the child are the cause of this harm, or the child is 'beyond parental control'.
3 Making an order is better for the child than making no order at all.

Of course, the legal framework is more complex than this list implies, and we devote considerable space in chapter 8 to examining the precise formulations that the Children Act 1989 has introduced. Moreover, despite the firm intention to overcome the historical legacies, in practical terms their influence will not be swept away at a stroke. Nevertheless, the Act does represent a radical departure from and improvement on the past, in terms of the legal mechanism by which state intervention can be enforced (see Box 1.1).

| BOX 1.1 | IMPROVEMENT IN THE PROCESS BY WHICH STATE INTERVENTION IS ENFORCED |

Rationalisation of the basis of decision-making

The shift to a single route for statutory intervention, on the basis of a single set of grounds and principles which are explicitly stated, represents a major simplification. It means that the system is much easier for everybody to understand, easier for professionals to operate and easier for parents to challenge.

The welfare checklist must be applied, in order that the decision is based on a consideration of all aspects of the child's circumstances and the child's ascertainable wishes and feelings are taken into account. Directions appointments and written reports, made available to the court and parties prior to the hearing, enable decision-making to be better-informed and avoid the need for cases to be adjourned.

Opening up decision-making

The power to transfer parenthood to the state is now located exclusively within the courts. Social services no longer have the authority to assume parental rights in closed meetings with little accountability. They must make a case in open court, with the child's parents (and others with parental responsibility) entitled to be present, and with a Guardian ad Litem to represent the child's interests. The child is also entitled to be legally represented.

Exploring other options

It is no longer sufficient to satisfy the grounds for making an order. The local authority must also satisfy the court that taking the child into care is the best (or the least harmful) outcome that can be achieved, by presenting the court with their plans for the child's upbringing and care. The court will usually compare this care plan with the likely outcome of other options, such as making a Residence Order to allow a relative to take on the child's upbringing.

Speeding up the process

The 'no delay' principle [s1(2)] is aided by the court's powers to set timetables and make directions over the provision of written information prior to the hearing. These are intended to avoid cases being drawn out.

Changes in the way intervention works

During the passage of the Children Act there was very little discussion of Supervision Orders, which were generally regarded as uncontroversial. However, some improvements have been made. These include the rationalisation of the grounds on which an order can be made for welfare purposes (the Children and Young Persons Act 1969 criminal supervision provisions remain in force, with some minor modifications) and considerable clarification of the impact the order has, not just upon the child or young person but also their parent(s). The child's parent(s) retain full parental responsibility, but may be asked to agree to comply with certain requirements made by the court and with directions given by the person appointed as the supervisor (see *responsible person* in the glossary).

The main criticism of the care system prior to the 1989 Children Act was that it usually left children and parents with very little say in decision-making and it tended to set children adrift, cutting them off from their parents, wider family and community. Children were left prey to changing fashions in residential care policy and usually given little choice about what

17

kind of arrangements were made. All too often their position was unclear, and local authorities themselves were muddled about the limits of their authority. Again, while it will take a lot more than legislative change to bring about improvements, the Act does set out to redress these problems and clarify lines of authority (see Box 1.2).

BOX 1.2	IMPROVEMENT IN THE OPERATION OF STATE INTERVENTION

Parents retain involvement in the child's upbringing

On the making of a Care Order, the local authority gains parental responsibility for the child and, to all intents and purposes, takes on the role of parent. However, the child's parents do not lose parental responsibility, although they will be severely limited in the extent to which they can exercise it – they will have no legal authority to act in ways which compromise the plans that the local authority has made for the child and its execution of those plans. Nevertheless, they must continue to be consulted in all significant decisions made about the child's upbringing, be positively encouraged to participate in the child's upbringing, and their contact with the child must be fostered.

Giving children a voice

The Act specifically requires local authorities to ascertain the wishes and feelings of children with regard to the arrangements made for their care, and to involve children as active participants in the regular reviews that must be held. It obliges local authorities to set up and administer effective complaints procedures. Moreover it offers children (with leave of the court) access to another legal route out of care, via a Residence Order, so that they can, for example, go to live with a relative instead.

Clarification of the child's status

Under the Act, a child is either quite specifically 'in care' (with all that this implies about who can exercise parental responsibility) or not. No longer are there vague divisions between 'voluntary' and 'compulsory' care, which frequently left those looking after the child – and often the child and parents too – uncertain about the limits of their authority.

Using this book

In this chapter we have touched on some of the main principles which underpin child welfare legislation. The remainder of the book takes up these themes and expands upon them, showing in practical terms how they operate and are applied.

There remains one important point to make before moving on to this more detailed examination. It is that the Children Act was designed as a whole and is intended to be read and used as such. That is, while its various sections address various aspects of children's welfare, they cannot simply be isolated from each other – they mesh together and depend upon each other. As an example, it is impossible to make sense of the specific provisions for child protection without referring to the provision of welfare services – a critical component in preventing child mistreatment and in avoiding the need for enforced statutory intervention. Thus it is important to avoid the temptation to flick through the book and assume you can just pick out those parts that apply directly to you. To do so would be to get a very partial picture and to miss out on certain facts which will be highly relevant to you.

At the same time, the world being what it is, the various other forms of legislation do not always fit as neatly as we might hope. For example, the provisions of the Criminal Justice Act 1991 relating to children's evidence in criminal proceedings are, in some ways, difficult to reconcile with the provisions of the Children Act for conducting child protection investigations. In this context too, it is critical not to skip over the parts which may seem less salient. Where we have included other legislation in the book, it is because it has direct relevance to children's welfare.

A final plea is to persuade you of the importance of the last chapter. The opportunity to ask fundamental questions about the impact of law and consider whether the law actually does any good is valuable. We think it does – we would hardly have written the book if we did not.

We believe that children and young people are entitled to certain basic rights – to be treated with respect; to be listened to and taken seriously; to participate to the full extent of their capacity in the decisions made and actions taken on their behalf. They are entitled both to be protected from harm and to receive the love, care and opportunities that will enable them to flourish. To us, the most important purpose of the law is to foster these rights. If this book can help parents and professionals (and indeed all those with children's interests at heart) to do that, then we will feel that it has been worthwhile.

2 Child welfare law: how the legal system operates

This chapter examines child welfare law in general terms. It describes the main features of the Children Act 1989 and uses this to illustrate how the law operates. We have included some very basic information about how law gets made, how it works and how it is disseminated, because many people who work with and care for children may have never learned about these. If you are familiar with these aspects, you may find you can skim over some parts quite quickly.

HOW THE LAW GETS MADE

The law is produced by two main processes: through legislation being passed by Parliament (usually called statute law), and by rulings made by courts (usually called case law). Sometimes the term 'common law' is used for established, traditional case law.

Case law

Case law stems from judgements made in the High Court, Court of Appeal or House of Lords (the highest court of all). Their decisions are binding on lower courts. An example is the Gillick Appeal ruling, made in 1986 by the House of Lords, which overturned the decision of a lower court (The Court of Appeal). This House of Lords ruling established, as a precedent (that is, a principle in law), that young people are entitled, in some circumstances, to make decisions for themselves once they gain sufficient age and maturity to make an informed decision. An example of common law is the 'inherent jurisdiction of the High Court', under which judges in the High Court had, up until the

Children Act, virtually limitless powers to make orders 'in the best interests of the child'. The best known is making the child a ward of court (wardship). The Children Act [s100] now limits the availability of these powers as far as local authorities are concerned, restricting them to those situations where there is no statutory remedy.

Statute law

The Education Act 1981, the Children Act 1989 and the Criminal Justice Act 1991 are all examples of statute law which wholly or in part legislate over children's welfare. New legislation of this kind may be made as a direct consequence of plans set out in a party manifesto, put in motion once they form a government. Other legislation stems from the work of the Law Commission or a Parliamentary Select Committee. Individual Members of Parliament can, in theory, also instigate legislation although, in practice, it will require the support of the Government to become law.

The passage of an Act of Parliament

Legislation is put before Parliament in the form of a bill, which must then be passed through a number of stages in both Houses of Parliament before it can become law. In its first reading, the bill is formally introduced to Parliament. At its second reading, its general principles are debated and voted on. Then follows a committee stage, where each clause is debated and voted on by a committee, outside of the main business of Parliament. A report of these deliberations is written and this report is then considered by Parliament once more, when further changes may be made to individual clauses. At its third reading, the bill, as amended, is debated and a final vote taken. Finally, the Monarch gives royal assent to the Bill, which then becomes law as an Act of Parliament.

Implementation

This does not end the matter – the legislation still has to be enacted, and this is by no means automatic. The Children Act 1989 gained royal assent in late 1989, but the major part of it was not implemented until October 1991. The reason for the delay was to allow sufficient time for training, for those affected (e.g. local authorities and the courts) to make the changes necessary for implementation, and for the drawing up of the necessary 'subordinate instruments'.

SECONDARY LEGISLATION

An Act of Parliament is usually referred to as the 'primary legislation', as it is a record of the law which has been through the full rigours of the parliamentary process. Just as important (and with equal force in law) is the 'secondary legislation' which goes with it. This is usually drawn up after royal assent has been given, and spells out the precise detail of how the legislation is to be applied in practice. The secondary legislation is set out in documents of two main kinds: Rules of Court and Regulations.

Rules of Court

The Rules of Court specify precise arrangements for how the court-based parts of the legislation will work. For example, the Children Act statute says that an application for an Emergency Protection Order may be made to a court. The Rules of Court then spell out in detail how and to whom an application for an Emergency Protection Order can be made, depending on particular circumstances. For example, they stipulate that 'out of hours' an application may be made to a single magistrate, but only with the permission of the Justices' Clerk.

Regulations

Regulations, which have the full force of law, supply detailed instructions about those parts of the legislation which relate to practice outside of the court system. Usually written together with Guidance, Regulations specify such things as the precise arrangements that must be made to register child-minders, the frequency with which reviews must be held concerning children who are being 'looked after', and so on.

Guidance

Guidance documents set out expectations about the way the legislation should be used to bring about the purposes it was designed to achieve and, more generally, the instructions of central government (the relevant ministries) for 'good practice' at local level. The Guidance documents for the Children Act explain how the legislation is intended to work, discuss its implications for policy and practice, and identify areas where particular attention may need to be paid. Guidance does not have the same force in law as Regulations, but, nonetheless, it is worth noting that Guidance is far from discretionary:

> *Though they are not in themselves law in the way that regulations are law, guidance documents are likely to be quoted or used in court proceedings as well as in local authority policy and practice papers. They could provide the basis for a legal challenge of an authority's action or inaction, including (in extreme cases) default action by the Secretary of State.*
> (*The Care of Children*, Department of Health, 1990).

Thus, although the Guidance is not law, local authorities and other public bodies will be wise to comply with the principles of good practice that they lay out.

THE CHILDREN ACT 1989

The Children Act is extremely wide-ranging in that it covers both public and private law in relation to children and includes extensive provisions concerning cases brought to court, as well as setting out the functions of public bodies and regulating how these must be performed.

Like most large Acts of Parliament, it is divided into *Sections* and *Schedules*, both of which have equal force and significance in law. In general terms, the Schedules deal with the more nitty-gritty detail and with amendments to previous legislation, whereas the Sections address the substantive body of law.

General principles

The Children Act begins by setting out general principles about how decisions should be made in court proceedings. Section 1 directs the court to make the child's welfare its 'paramount consideration' [s1(1)], to avoid delay [s1(2)], and not to make orders 'unless it considers that doing so would be better for the child than making no order at all' [s1(5)]. It also provides a checklist (usually referred to as the 'welfare checklist') of issues the court should consider when deciding on matters to do with a child's upbringing (including care proceedings). This is set out in Box 2.1.

BOX 2.1   THE WELFARE CHECKLIST

The 'welfare checklist' [s1(3)] lists the following that the court must take into account in making decisions:

1   the ascertainable wishes and feelings of the child concerned (considered in the light of the child's age and understanding);

2   the child's physical, emotional and educational needs;

3   the likely effect on the child of any change in circumstances;

4   the child's age, sex, background and any characteristics which the court considers relevant;

5   any harm the child has suffered, or is at risk of suffering;

6   how capable each of the child's parents, and any other person in relation to whom the court considers the question to be relevant, is of meeting his or her needs;

7   the range of powers available to the court under this Act in the proceedings in question.

This checklist applies to all contested applications for making, varying or discharging section 8 orders and all applications for Care and Supervision Orders, Education Supervision Orders and for contact with children in care.

Other general principles are included in the body of the Act. These are summarised in Box 2.2.

BOX 2.2   MAIN PRINCIPLES OF THE CHILDREN ACT

The Children Act 1989 is intended to promote a number of important principles. These can be thought of as the philosophy behind the Act, and are always important to take into account whenever considering any particular part of the Act.

1   The welfare of the child or young person must be the paramount consideration in any decision made or action taken.

2   Children and young people are entitled to be protected if they are in danger of suffering significant harm, although such intervention must be open to challenge.

3   Wherever possible, children and young people should be brought up and cared for by their own families.

4   Parents whose children are in need (including all children who are disabled) should be helped to bring up their children themselves.

5   This help should be offered as a service to the child and the family, and draw on effective collaboration between agencies, including those in the voluntary sector. It should be provided in partnership with parents, meet the child's identified needs and be appropriate in terms of the child's race, culture, religion and linguistic background. There must be an effective independent complaints procedure.

6   The state cannot enforce intervention unless there are serious shortcomings in the care given to children by their parents and the child is at risk of significant harm. Local authorities cannot acquire parental responsibility for a child or young person without a court order.

7   When a child or young person has no parents, or where parents cannot offer their children adequate standards of care, high quality substitute care must be provided.

8   Children and young people must be consulted and kept informed about actions taken, and participate in decisions made about them.

9 Situations where a child or young person lives away from home must be open to scrutiny, to make sure adequate standards of care and safety are maintained.

10 Parents and the wider family continue to have a role in the lives of children and young people, even when they live apart from them. Contact with their family should be fostered wherever possible.

Local authority duties and powers

Legislation like the Children Act, when specifying the functions of a public body such as a local authority, is generally divided between two kinds of statement – about their duties and their powers. It is important to recognise the fundamental difference between them.

A duty sets out something which they are *obliged* to do and is generally recognisable by the word 'shall'. So, for example, when the Act states that 'Every local authority shall open and maintain a register of disabled children within their area' [Sched 2(2)], this is a duty which they *must* fulfil. Often such obligations are hedged around by saying they shall 'take what steps they consider to be reasonable'. (There will undoubtedly be challenges about whether or not they have complied, in specific circumstances.) However, they cannot be completely ignored. If they are, local authorities may be called to account (e.g. by way of judicial review).

A power confers discretion, *allowing* something to be done, and can usually be identified by the word 'may'. This can be seen when Schedule 2(2) goes on to state that 'The register may be kept by means of a computer'. This means they can – but do not have to – computerise the register.

Judicial review

A judicial review can be sought when it is believed that, for example, a government minister or a local authority has done something they are not authorised to do, misinterpreted the law, ignored a procedural requirement or abused their powers, all in relation to a particular statute. In some circumstances the issue may be more one of generally breaching the principles of natural justice or failing to act fairly. Applicants must be persons who are affected by the statute in question.

The action or decision will not, itself, be considered, but whether or not it was properly arrived at. The outcome, if the court finds that there has been an error, may be simply to point this out, although usually the court will direct that it is rectified and may in some circumstances award damages.

Court orders

The Act specifies the orders that a court can make and, for each one, designates who may apply, what grounds or conditions need to be fulfilled before the order can be made, the powers and duties which are mandated by the order, how long it can last, and how the order may be discharged (that is, be brought to an end) or varied (that is, altered).

Similar in form are warrants, which may be provided to the police to empower them to take a particular action (e.g. enter a house and search for a child).

Definitions

Sometimes – but by no means always – legislation defines its terms, in order to ensure that its intentions are clearly understood. *Harm*, for example, is defined in the Children Act as 'ill-treatment or the impairment of health or development' [s31(9)]. Thereafter, *development* is defined as meaning 'physical, intellectual, emotional or behavioural development'; *health* as 'physical or mental health'; and *ill-treatment* as including 'sexual abuse and forms of ill-treatment which are not physical'.

Other terms, however, have been left undefined, to allow courts discretion to take into account the particular factors of each case. Whereas in the Children Act the term 'significant harm' is critical for determining whether a court may make certain orders, the term 'significant' is not defined in the Act itself. It will be a question of fact for the court to decide, although the *Guidance and Regulations* [Vol 1, para 3.21] do flesh this out somewhat (see chapter 8 for more details).

Referring directly to the Act

The Children Act does, in the main, use ordinary language and avoids legal jargon. You should refer directly to the Act whenever you want to know exactly what the law says, rather than relying on commentaries or interpretations which may introduce distortions. This can be done by looking at the Act itself or by using one of the several books which include a copy of the Act.

Children Act Guidance and Regulations

For the Children Act, nine separate volumes of *Guidance and Regulations* were produced, covering different areas of the legislation. (Full references for these are listed at the end of the book under Further Reading). They are overlapping in content, in that each is designed to be used on its own and is self-contained. The intention is that all practitioners working in a particular sphere (such as day care) should have access to the relevant volume of *Guidance and Regulations* (in this case, Volume 2) so that they know precisely where they stand over any aspect of their work which is at issue.

Other Guidance documents

The Care of Children: Principles and Practice in Regulations and Guidance (Department of Health, 1990) provides a general overview of the principles of good child care which underpin the Children Act. It is aimed primarily at social services departments, but is of general use to anybody with responsibility for children's welfare.

Working Together under the Children Act 1989: A Guide to the Arrangements for Inter-agency Co-operation for the Protection of Children from Abuse (Department of Health and Welsh Office,

1991) replaces an earlier document on the same subject and is intended to offer overall guidelines for all the agencies involved in child protection work. It sets out principles of good practice for co-operation and collaboration, and explains how these can be achieved within the new legislative framework provided by the Act.

CHANGES IN THE LAW

Taken together, the Children Act itself, its Rules of Court and Guidance and Regulations comprise the formal, explicit statement of the legislation. They cannot, however, be taken as the last word, since the law undergoes constant change. This happens in three main ways.

Changes by way of case law

Once an Act is implemented, its provisions – and especially the way it is interpreted – are open to challenge in the courts. We can expect to see, as time goes by, a number of rulings in the higher courts which will have a significant impact on the Act.

Changes in secondary legislation

Guidance and Regulations can be amended and updated to take account of events and reactions. In 1993 the Department of Health issued new Regulations and Guidance about the management of 'difficult behaviour' in children and young people living in residential establishments. Concerns had been raised by staff working in such establishments. They were finding that the Act's provisions were not working very well and requested clarification. The new Regulations modified the instructions that had been provided previously and spelt out in greater detail what staff could and could not do in certain situations (see chapter 8 for more details). Other changes have also been made, including in respect to day care. It is therefore important to keep constantly abreast of the current situation, since such changes are an ongoing process.

New legislation

New legislation can completely repeal previous law, although it is unlikely to happen to the Children Act in the foreseeable future.

It can, however, have a considerable impact. This has happened as a result of the Child Support Act 1991 and the setting up of the Child Support Agency. These have largely removed from courts the powers given to them by a number of statutes, including the Children Act, to decide the amount of maintenance that should be paid for children after parental separation.

At least as important is the way new legislation, while not directly affecting existing law, can, by coming alongside it, quite seriously alter the way it works in practice. This is illustrated well by the way that the children's evidence provisions of the Criminal Justice Act 1991 have had a noticeable impact on the way local authorities go about investigating allegations of child abuse. We will consider this in detail in chapter 5.

LOCAL POLICY AND PROCEDURES

Legislation and its associated Guidance can only ever offer generalised advice and instructions. For law to be put into practice effectively, local policy must be devised and procedure documents prepared which take account of local conditions and existing local arrangements. For example, local authorities are required by law to devise complaints procedures. Guidance and Regulations indicate the general scope of what must be done. It is, however, left up to those responsible in each area to decide how complaints procedures will work in their authority, to devise procedures, write them up and distribute them.

Local policies and procedures must conform to what is set out in the legislation and must follow established principles of good practice (such as set out in *The Care of Children*). However, there is a fair amount of leeway in terms of precise detail. The overall aim of these documents is to make sure that staff (and, where appropriate, others like voluntary workers) have a clear understanding of precisely what is expected of them. They set out their responsibilities and the extent and limits of their authority. They specify what action is to be taken in certain circumstances (like when a child is injured), in what timescale, and whom they must consult or inform.

In some cases, policy documents and procedures will be a simple expansion and setting out of the practicalities of a particular bit of legislation. In other cases, though, their production will be the result of having grappled with the inter-relationships between different legal statutes, as in the interface between the Children Act and the Criminal Justice Act. Some will be produced within a single agency, others will need to be negotiated between a number of agencies. *Working Together under the Children Act 1989* prescribes that this should be done by Area Child Protection Committees (ACPCs), although the task is usually undertaken by a smaller sub-group who draft the procedures and bring them back to the ACPC for ratification.

THE COURT SYSTEM

Matters concerning children's welfare, both in terms of private and public law, are dealt with by civil courts in what are called civil proceedings. However, where children are victims of and/or witnesses to crimes (such as when there is an allegation that a child has been sexually abused), the child may also be involved in criminal proceedings. Later in this chapter, we will look at the ways that criminal proceedings may have an impact on civil proceedings.

The Children Act and its Rules of Court created a new civil court system to deal with children's cases, consisting of three levels of court (see Figure 2.1).

A new Family Proceedings Court was set up at the Magistrates' level, drawing its magistrates from those who had served in either Juvenile or Domestic Courts. These Family Proceedings Courts now deal with the majority of cases under the Act. The idea is that, because these courts are local, they should be more accessible to all those involved in the case and, together with the ability to move cases around in a locality, this means that cases can be dealt with more rapidly and conveniently for all involved.

All three levels of court have concurrent jurisdiction with more or less equal powers (i.e. save for a few exceptions, they can all make the same orders). The information brought before them has

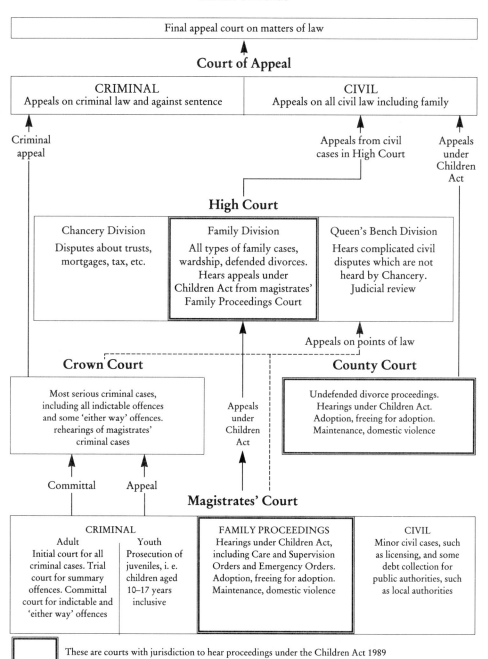

House of Lords

Final appeal court on matters of law

Court of Appeal

CRIMINAL	CIVIL
Appeals on criminal law and against sentence	Appeals on all civil law including family

Criminal appeal

Appeals from civil cases in High Court

Appeals under Children Act

High Court

Chancery Division	Family Division	Queen's Bench Division
Disputes about trusts, mortgages, tax, etc.	All types of family cases, wardship, defended divorces. Hears appeals under Children Act from magistrates' Family Proceedings Court	Hears complicated civil disputes which are not heard by Chancery. Judicial review

Appeals on points of law

Crown Court

Most serious criminal cases, including all indictable offences and some 'either way' offences. rehearings of magistrates' criminal cases

Appeals under Children Act

County Court

Undefended divorce proceedings. Hearings under Children Act. Adoption, freeing for adoption. Maintenance, domestic violence

Committal   Appeal

Magistrates' Court

CRIMINAL		FAMILY PROCEEDINGS	CIVIL
Adult Initial court for all criminal cases. Trial court for summary offences. Committal court for indictable and 'either way' offences	Youth Prosecution of juveniles, i. e. children aged 10–17 years inclusive	Hearings under Children Act, including Care and Supervision Orders and Emergency Orders. Adoption, freeing for adoption. Maintenance, domestic violence	Minor civil cases, such as licensing, and some debt collection for public authorities, such as local authorities

These are courts with jurisdiction to hear proceedings under the Children Act 1989

Figure 2.1 The court system

been standardised (using standard application forms and written reports), so that cases can be transferred with relative ease where the need arises (e.g. where a case takes on added complexity).

Allocation and transfer of cases

Disputes about arrangements for children following parental divorce or separation can be heard in any of the three courts. Public law proceedings will generally be heard in Magistrates' Courts, except where:

- the case is exceptionally grave, important or complex – for example, where the evidence is complicated or where there may be conflict with the jurisdiction of another country;
- other proceedings concerning the child are already in progress in another court;
- a move to another court will significantly reduce delay.

Decision-making in court

Especially at the Magistrates' level, the approach of the court has been changed by altering the role that the court plays. Previously, the court tended to be somewhat passive, listening to the cases being made by the two sides and determining whether or not the grounds for an order had been proved (and, if so, making the order). Following the Act, however, the court has become more active. It now sees itself as looking for 'the best resolution' by, for example, actively seeking information about the range of possible outcomes that might be achieved and working out what (if any) orders can be made to achieve them. For example, the court has the power to make a different order from that applied for.

– KAREN'S STORY –

Nine-month-old Karen has been placed in foster care, following an Emergency Protection Order sought by the local authority because her leg had been broken by her mother. Karen's injuries were such that the doctor concluded they were very unlikely to be the result of an accident, but had been caused deliberately. Karen's mother admitted to the doctor she had 'lost control' and twisted Karen's leg when she was changing her nappy.

The local authority subsequently apply for a Care Order, because they are worried about returning Karen to the care of her mother. Karen's mother contests the order, saying she has learned her lesson and she will not harm the baby again. The Guardian ad Litem appointed by the court prepares a report suggesting that Karen's welfare would best be served by going to live, for the time being at least, with her grandparents, with her mother able to visit regularly.

The magistrates will have a number of options. They could make no order and simply return Karen to her parents. Indeed, they are required to do this unless they are convinced that making an order is best for the baby [s1(5)]. They could allow the child to return home but make a Supervision Order, with, for example, directions specifying that a social worker will visit the family at frequent intervals and that Karen must attend a family centre with her mother each day. They could make the Care Order as the local authority have requested or they could, as the Guardian suggests, make a Residence Order in the grandparents' favour, directing that Karen go to live with them, and a Contact Order setting out that her mother can see her there.

Guardian ad Litem

The Guardian ad Litem is an officer of the court, appointed in most public law proceedings to represent the child's interests and provide an independent viewpoint about what outcome is likely to be best for the child. Guardians have a number of powers (such as access to records) and duties (such as instructing a solicitor to represent the court, if this has not already been done). They are expected to attend all directions appointments and hearings, and to keep the child informed about what is going on.

The Guardian ad Litem is expected to advise the court on:

- whether the child is of sufficient age and experience to

consent to a medical examination, and whether or not the child should attend the hearing(s);

- the wishes of the child about matters the court is considering;
- the appropriate forum and timing of proceedings;
- the different outcomes which may be achieved, and which one is likely to be best for the child;
- any other matters the Guardian or the court sees as relevant.

In care proceedings, the Guardian will prepare a detailed report and submit this to the court prior to the main hearing. The Guardian is intended to be independent and therefore cannot be an employee of the local authority which is party to the proceedings (or the NSPCC, if it is) except if specifically employed as a member of a Guardian ad Litem panel. The Guardian also must not be or have been an employee of a local authority or voluntary agency who has been directly involved in the care of the child in the past five years, or a probation officer who has worked with the child or the family.

Directions appointments

An important innovation introduced by the Children Act is that some time before certain proceedings (e.g. care proceedings) a 'directions appointment' will usually be held. All the parties (and/or their representatives) in the case are expected to attend. In the Magistrates' Court this is usually run by the Justices' Clerk. Its purpose is to set a timetable for the proceedings and to make directions about the following:

- the appointment of a Guardian ad Litem (if this has not already been done);
- whether or not the child will attend the hearing;
- what documents will be submitted and when these will be served on the other parties;
- what evidence will be submitted, including experts' reports;
- the preparation of welfare reports.

The overall aim is to clarify, as far as possible, the main thrust of the arguments that will be made and the evidence that will be presented, ahead of the actual hearing. In this way it is expected that, when the case does come to court, it will be able to run as smoothly as possible, without the need for adjournments and with all the information available that the court needs in order to make a well-informed judgement.

CRIMINAL PROCEEDINGS

Criminal proceedings are not covered by the Children Act or other child welfare law. Our interest in them is that a child who, for example, has been assaulted may appear as a witness in the prosecution of the alleged offender. The Criminal Justice Act 1991 has introduced changes which can, in specified circumstances, enable children to give their evidence-in-chief by way of a pre-recorded video-taped interview, which will usually be conducted jointly by a specially trained social worker and police officer. A *Memorandum of Good Practice* (Home Office/Department of Health, 1992) has been issued, offering guidelines about how such interviews should be conducted.

– MARK'S STORY –

Mark is eight. At school his teacher heard him tell another boy his bottom was sore. When she asked him what was wrong, he said 'It's rude. It's a secret. I can't tell you.' When she tries to get him to say more, Mark becomes very upset. The school contact social services. A social worker and a police officer come to the school. After talking to the head and the teacher, they decide they should interview Mark.

Their local protocol on joint investigation says they must 'keep their options open' for prosecuting the person suspected of abusing the child. To do this they will need to jointly interview Mark, following the *Memorandum of Good Practice*, and record the interview on video-tape. They face a number of dilemmas, such as whether to inform Mark's mother and whether to seek her consent to the interview. What should they tell Mark? How far can they explain to him what is going on?

Mark's case illustrates the tensions between the welfare provisions of the Children Act and the implications of possible criminal proceedings. The best course of action for protecting Mark may be to work as closely as possible with his parents and to seek his informed co-operation, but this may well not be the best approach for gaining evidence for criminal proceedings. To see why this is so, we need to consider how criminal proceedings differ from civil proceedings. The dilemmas themselves will be taken up in chapter 5.

Differences between civil and criminal proceedings

Civil and criminal law differ in a number of fundamental ways. The main differences are summarised in Figure 2.2.

	Civil proceedings	Criminal proceedings
Burden of proof	The plaintiff	The prosecution
Standards of proof	Balance of probabilities	Beyond reasonable doubt
Grounds for making orders	The child is or is likely to be at risk of significant harm	The accused committed the alleged offence
Competence of the child witness	The child understands he or she must speak the truth	Child assumed to be competent
Attendance of child in court	Child's wishes and welfare likely to determine whether or not he or she attends	If child's testimony is to be considered, the child must attend at least for cross-examination, but this may be by video-link
Rules of evidence	'Relaxed' – generally hearsay rules do not apply	Apply except in some specified circumstances
Video recording of evidence	Generally admissible	May replace the child's evidence-in-chief if the child can be cross-examined

Figure 2.2   Comparison between civil and criminal procedures

The burden of proof
The burden of proof is to do with which side in a court case has to prove certain matters. In a civil case it is the plaintiff (i.e. the person bringing the action, such as the local authority or the parent applying for the order) that usually bears the burden of proof. In a criminal case it is generally the prosecution (i.e. the crown).

Standards of proof

The standard of proof refers to the criterion for making judgements in legal proceedings, and concerns the degree of certainty that magistrates, judges or juries should consider in making their judgements. In civil proceedings concerning children's welfare (e.g. in care proceedings) the standard of proof is 'on the balance of probabilities' (i.e. that it is more likely than not that the events alleged to have occurred did in fact occur). The standard of proof in a criminal trial, however, is much more strict – the case against the accused must be proved 'beyond reasonable doubt'. This means that, if there is any doubt in the minds of the jury, they should acquit the accused.

Basically, what this difference amounts to is that in civil proceedings the court can decide to intervene (e.g. to make a Care Order to protect the child) once certain facts have been established as proved 'on the balance of probabilities'. In contrast, a criminal court cannot convict a person unless it is established 'beyond reasonable doubt' that the accused committed a specific offence.

Grounds for making orders

In civil proceedings for child protection, grounds for making orders generally centre around establishing that the child is suffering or likely to suffer 'significant harm', which is attributable to a failure of parental care or because the child is deemed as being beyond parental control. (This is discussed in more detail in chapters 5 and 8). The focus of evidence is upon the *risks to the child*. In criminal proceedings, however, what has to be established is that the accused committed a specified offence. The focus of evidence here, therefore, is upon the *actions of the accused*.

In civil proceedings (such as an application for a Care Order), all that may be necessary in Mark's case will be to convince the court, on the balance of probabilities, that Mark has been significantly harmed and that without a court order he is at risk of further significant harm. Were this same case to reach a criminal trial of Mark's father for sexually assaulting him, then, for Mark's father to be convicted, it must be established beyond all reasonable doubt that it was he who sexually assaulted Mark. Thus it is perfectly possible in a case like Mark's for the child to be placed in the care of the local authority, even though nobody has been convicted of a specific offence towards him.

Competence of the child witness

As far as civil proceedings are concerned, a child may be called as a witness and give unsworn evidence if, in the opinion of the court, the child understands that he or she must speak the truth and has sufficient understanding to justify his or her evidence being heard [s96(1 & 2)]. In criminal proceedings, the provisions of the Criminal Justice Act 1991 specify that a child witness is to be treated as competent to testify, unless shown otherwise. Unlike adults, children under fourteen need not take the oath, but their testimony will be considered as if they had. Where, however, a child (and indeed any witness) proves to be unable to give a comprehensible account of events, that child's evidence will not be able to form part of either the prosecution or defence case.

The child's attendance in court

In civil proceedings the court can order the child to attend a particular stage of the court proceedings [s95]. However, courts are generally unwilling to force a child to attend, unless the child is willing to appear and this is considered in his or her best interests. The Guardian ad Litem will be expected to consider this question carefully and advise the court on this matter.

In criminal proceedings the child's testimony may be critical to the prosecution. The case may therefore not go ahead unless the child can appear as a witness. The child may testify in person or by way of a live video-link (where the child sits in a room next to the court, set up with technical equipment which allows the court to see and hear the child, and the child to see and hear whoever is questioning them). In some circumstances the child's main evidence (evidence-in-chief) may be given in the form of a video-taped interview (as described above). The video recording will not, however, be admissible unless the child is available for cross-examination, although the accused will not be able to cross-examine the child in person and the cross-examination may be conducted via live video-link.

Rules concerning the child's evidence

In civil proceedings, as the rules over hearsay (see glossary) have been relaxed, oral and written reports of what a child has said and video recordings of interviews with children may be submitted as evidence. In criminal proceedings, hearsay and all other rules about evidence *do apply*, both to the child's evidence-in-chief (whether given in court, by live video-link or by way of a pre-recorded interview) and to cross-examination. Whilst these rules regarding evidence and its admissibility have been and are complicated, the idea of evidence is simple – it refers to those matters which have to be established or proved in order to make a case. There is a very useful breakdown of the legal elements – what has to be proved – of the main sexual and violent offences in Annex D to the *Memorandum of Good Practice*.

There are three rules of evidence which the *Memorandum of Good Practice* identifies as being of particular importance in criminal proceedings – those concerning leading questions; previous statements; and statements about the bad character of the accused. Together these rules impose restrictions on the way a child can be interviewed (see chapter 5 for more details).

3 *Parenthood and disputes about children's upbringing*

In this chapter we will examine the notion of parenthood and what, in law, it implies in terms of rights and responsibilities. We will also look at the Children Act's provisions for resolving disputes about a child's upbringing. While these will generally be most relevant when parents divorce or separate, we will see that they may sometimes apply in other circumstances, such as when a child is taken into 'care' or where another person outside the family wants to challenge some aspect of a child's care. In some circumstances children and young people may, themselves, seek to intervene in their own upbringing.

WHO IS A PARENT?

At first, this might seem a strange question to pose. However, in the light of recent advances in medical technology, the answer is no longer as straightforward as it once was.

Who is a child's legal mother?

Normally, the woman who gives birth to a child is, in law, the child's mother. However, where the child is born as a result of *in vitro* fertilisation, the position is less clear. Now, under the Human Fertilisation and Embryology Act 1990, the 'woman who is carrying or has carried a child as a result of the placing in her of an embryo or of sperm and eggs, and no other woman, is to be treated as the mother of the child' [s27(1)]. The exceptions to this are:

1   where an application is made by a married couple for an
    order under the Human Fertilisation and Embryology Act
    1990 [s30], the court is empowered to make an order
    providing for a child to be treated in law as the child of the
    parties to the marriage. This applies to circumstances where
    the child was carried by a woman other than the wife, as the
    result of the placing in her of an embryo or sperm and eggs
    or her artificial insemination following the use of gametes of
    one or both of the spouses;
2   where the child is subsequently adopted.

Thus a woman can become the mother of a child in one of three
ways: by giving birth to that child; by a court order under the
Human Fertilisation and Embryology Act 1990; or by adopting
the child (adoption is dealt with, briefly, in chapter 8).

Who is a child's legal father?

This is even more complicated. The general rule is that the
genetic father (i.e. the person who 'fathered' the child) is the legal
father, but there are two exceptions to this. There are also
instances when a man will be treated as the father even though
there is no genetic link. The two exceptions to the general rule
are contained in section 28(6) of the Human Fertilisation and
Embryology Act 1990. A genetic father is not, in law, held to be
the child's legal father when:

1   he is a donor whose sperm has been used for 'licensed
    treatment' and whose consent has been obtained in
    accordance with the provisions of the Human Fertilisation
    and Embryology Act 1990;
2   his sperm is used after his death.

In contrast, where a child is born to a married woman as a result
of 'artificial insemination by donor' (AID), the child will be
presumed, in law, to be the child of the father as well as the
mother, unless it can be shown that the husband did not consent
to the AID [s27 Family Law Reform Act 1987]. There is a
corresponding provision in the Human Fertilisation and
Embryology Act 1990 in relation to other forms of assisted

reproduction. Therefore, where a husband consents to any licensed medical intervention by which his wife is made pregnant with the sperm of another man, he will be the child's legal father. In the absence of his consent, however, in law the child will be fatherless.

Irrespective of this, the old common law rule is that, if a married couple have a child, the husband is presumed to be the child's father. This presumption can be rebutted – a man may claim paternity – but the standard of proof is high and the burden of proof falls on the man claiming to be the child's father. The entry of a man's name on the registration of the child's birth is viewed as strong but not conclusive evidence of paternity. For this it may be necessary to resort to medical testing.

Medical tests to establish parentage

Until the development of DNA 'genetic fingerprinting', the use of cruder forms of blood-testing was the only way in which parentage could be established or its presumption rebutted. However, while this kind of blood-test was able to establish that a person *could not be* the father, it could not prove conclusively that a particular man *was* the father. In contrast, recent medical advances have produced DNA testing, which does allow for the positive identification of the father. Tests of genetic paternity may be sought for a number of reasons, including when an application is made for financial relief in respect of a child of unmarried parents (discussed in more detail later in this chapter) and where an unmarried father is seeking to establish paternity in order to succeed in an application for a Parental Responsibility Order. In all cases the court has the discretion as to whether or not to order a test.

Unmarried fathers

Unmarried fathers, if known, are treated in law as fathers. This does not mean, however, that they automatically have parental responsibility in relation to a child. It does mean that they have certain obligations and legal responsibilities towards the child.

- The father has a legal responsibility to maintain or provide financial support for the child until he or she reaches adulthood or (if this is later) completes full-time education.

- The child has certain legal rights to inherit after the father's death.
- The father's conduct towards the child will be governed by legal restrictions with respect to marriage and incest.
- The father has an expectation of contact with the child if the child is in local authority care, unless the court orders to the contrary.

PARENTAL RESPONSIBILITY

Parental responsibility carries with it a number of obligations and the authority to act in certain ways (see Box 3.1).

BOX 3.1	WHAT DOES PARENTAL RESPONSIBILITY INVOLVE?

Independent Authority

The following are the most significant of the powers, rights, duties and responsibilities that parents have in relation to their children:

- a responsibility for the physical care and control of the child;
- the authority to discipline the child;
- a responsibility to maintain the child;
- a responsibility to ensure that the child receives an efficient full-time education suited to his or her needs and abilities;
- the authority to consent to the child being medically examined or to receive medical treatment;
- the authority to appoint a guardian (although a guardian will not acquire parental responsibility unless both parents are dead);
- an entitlement to be treated as a parent by the child's school, including being eligible to stand as a parent-governor.

All of these can be exercised independently of others who have parental responsibility for the child, unless there is a court order (e.g. a Care Order) which may have the effect of restricting one or more of these.

Authority which requires the consent of both parents who have parental responsibility

Other aspects of parental responsibility require the consent of both of the child's parents. These include:

- the authority to agree to the child being adopted;
- the authority to consent to the child getting married if the child is over the age of sixteen;
- the authority to remove the child from the UK.

Limits to parental authority towards 'mature minors'

The Gillick ruling (House of Lords ruling, Gillick v West Norfolk and Wisbech Area Health Authority, 1986) means that, while the parents have rights in order to allow them to promote and safeguard the welfare of their child, those rights are only exercisable in so far as they are needed to promote the child's welfare. As the child grows up they are gradually eclipsed by the child's right to make his or her own decisions.

HOW PARENTAL RESPONSIBILITY IS ACQUIRED

The different ways people can acquire and lose parental responsibility are summarised in Figure 3.1. The mother of a child automatically has parental responsibility. If the child's parents are married, the father also automatically has it. Married parents never lose responsibility for their children, unless the child is adopted or an order is made freeing the child for adoption. The fact that the marriage breaks down has no legal consequences affecting the parent–child relationship, and both parents will be able to act alone in the way they exercise parental responsibility for their child [s2(7)]. The same is true, in a more limited sense, for any other person who has acquired parental responsibility (e.g. by way of a Residence Order) or the local authority (e.g. by way of a Care Order). While the parent's authority to exercise parental responsibility will be limited by the order, the parent does not lose it entirely and retains a range of entitlements over things such as being consulted in decisions made about the child's upbringing (see Figure 3.1).

Person	How is parental responsibility obtained?	What they can or cannot do	Duration
Parent(s) (of a legitimate child) and the unmarried mother	Automatically	Can act independently in pursuance of parental responsibility [s2(7)], but not in a way which is incompatible with an order of the court [s2(8)]. Joint decision making is still required on matters specified in other statutes (See Box 3.1) [s2(7)]	Is not affected by divorce unless the court makes an order. Can only be brought to an end by the making of (1) an order declaring the child free for adoption, and (2) an adoption order
Guardian	By court order [s5(6)]. By appointment in writing or by will [s5(5)]	Has all the powers of a parent including the ability to appoint a guardian [s5(4)]	Brought to an end by court order on application of any person with parental responsibility, of the child with leave of the court, and in any family proceedings on court's own motion [s6(7)]. Ends when child reaches eighteen [s91(7) and (8)] or by written disclaimer [s6(5)]
Unmarried father	By court order on his application [s4(1) (a)]. (Where the unmarried father applies for and is granted a Residence Order, the court must make an order under section 4 [s12(1)]). By formal written agreement with mother [s4(1) (b)]. By being appointed a guardian [s5(6)]	As for parent(s) and unmarried mother	Brought to an end by court order on the application of any person who has parental responsibility for the child, or, with the leave of the court, the child [s4(3)]. Cannot be brought to an end while Residence Order in favour of unmarried father continues [ss4(3) & 12(4)]. Ends when the child reaches eighteen [s91(7) & (8)]
Non-parental holder of a Residence Order e.g. foster-parent or aunt	By court making a Residence Order [s12(2)]	Cannot consent to an order freeing for adoption, an Adoption Order [s12(3) (a) & (b)] or appoint a guardian for the child [s12(3) (c)]. When a Residence Order is in force, no person can change the child's surname or remove the child from the jurisdiction for a month or more without either leave of the court or written consent of all those with parental responsibility	While Residence Order is in force
Local authority	Under a Care Order [s33(3) (a)] or an order freeing the child for adoption [Sched 10, para 6]. Under an Emergency Protection Order (EPO) [s44(4) (c)]	Cannot consent to an order freeing for adoption, an Adoption Order [s33(6) (b)(i) & (ii) [appoint a guardian for the child [s33(6) (b)(iii)] or cause the child to be brought up in a different religion [s33(6) (a)]. Under an EPO, can only take such action in meeting its parental responsibility as is reasonably required to safeguard or promote the welfare of the child [s44(5) (b)]	While Care Order is in force Revocation of the freeing order returns parental responsibility to the parents [Sched 10, para 8], or it is brought to an end by the making of an Adoption Order. While the EPO is in force
Other applicant for an EPO	By court order [s44(4) (c)]	Can only exercise parental responsibility for the child as is reasonably required in order to safeguard or promote the welfare of the child [s44(5) (b)]	While the EPO is in force
Applicant under an Adoption Order	By court order [s12 Adoption Act 1976 as amended by Sched 10, para 3]. The order extinguishes the parental responsibility which any person had before the order was made and any order previously made under the Children Act 1989	Can act independently in pursuance of parental responsibility [s2(7)], but not in a way which is incompatible with an order of the court [s2(8)]	Is not affected by the divorce of the adoptive parents unless the court makes an order

Figure 3.1 Parental responsibility

How an unmarried father may gain parental responsibility

If the parents are not married to each other, there are four ways in which the unmarried father can, under the Children Act, acquire parental responsibility for the child:

1 apply to a court for a Parental Responsibility Order [s4(1)];
2 enter into a formal 'parental responsibility agreement' with the mother [s4(2)];
3 apply to a court for a Residence Order, in which case the court will also make a Parental Responsibility Order [s12(1)];
4 become the child's guardian on the mother's death [s5].

In addition, the unmarried father acquires parental responsibility for the child by subsequent marriage to the mother.

P ARENTAL RESPONSIBILITY ORDER [s4]

Who may apply? The child's father.

Welfare principle: The welfare checklist does not apply, but the presumption of no order [s1(5)] and paramountcy principle [s1(1)] do apply.

Powers and duties: The order confers parental responsibility for the child on the father, which he will then share with the mother.

Duration: The order lasts until the child reaches the age of eighteen, unless it is brought to an end.

Challenge: The order may be terminated by the court, on application by any person with parental responsibility, or (with leave) by the child.

When a father applies for a Parental Responsibility Order, although the court does not have to follow the welfare checklist, it is likely to want to consider the child's wishes if he or she is mature enough to express an informed view. More generally, the court will consider the character of the father and whether and to what extent he has played (and intends to play) a role in the child's upbringing. Given that, if the mother was agreeable to the idea of his having a legally recognised link with the child, they could make a parental responsibility agreement without the court intervening, the reasons for the father's application without the mother's co-operation are also likely to be taken into account. A lack of co-operation in itself, however, will not prevent an order being made.

How non-parents may gain parental responsibility

There are three main ways that somebody who is not the child's parent can acquire parental responsibility: by a Residence Order being made in their favour; on the death of the child's parents, by becoming the child's guardian; and by adoption.

Residence Orders

In principle, under the Children Act 1989 any adult person can acquire parental responsibility for a child by applying for a Residence Order [s12(2)]. In practice the courts will not make this order unless they are convinced that this is what is best for the child. In other words, courts will only give parental responsibility for a child to a person or persons who have an established and close relationship with the child and are realistically in a position to undertake the role of parenthood.

The Act recognises this commonsense approach by insisting that some applicants must seek the leave of the court before they are allowed to apply for a Residence Order, but giving other categories of person an automatic right to apply for a Residence Order without the leave of the court (see Box 3.2).

> ## BOX 3.2   WHO MAY APPLY FOR A RESIDENCE ORDER WITHOUT LEAVE OF THE COURT?
>
> The following are entitled to apply for a Residence Order without leave of the court:
>
> - the child's parent or guardian;
> - the husband or wife of the person who has parental responsibility for the child, where the child is a 'child of the family';
> - any person with whom the child has lived for at least three years (this need not be continuously, but must be within five years of the application);
> - any person with the permission of those holding an existing Residence Order or the permission of all of those with existing parental responsibility for the child;
> - any person with the permission of the local authority, where a child is in the care of the local authority – this includes foster-parents, even though the child has lived with them for less than three years.

Thus, in practice, it is possible for people like relatives, step-parents and foster-parents to acquire parental responsibility in circumstances where they can offer the child a more secure and stable upbringing than the child's parent(s). Others will be able to seek leave from the court to apply. The court must take into consideration the nature of the application, the applicant's connection with the child, and any risks of disruption which may harm the child. Where the child is in the care of the local authority, the court must also consider the local authority's plans for the child and the wishes and feelings of the child's parents [s10(9)]. The aim is to provide a flexible system that can be responsive to different circumstances, while preventing unwarranted incursions into a child's life.

Guardianship

Parents who have parental responsibility for a child may appoint another person to be a child's guardian in the event of their death [s5(3)], and guardians may appoint another person to become a guardian in the event of their death [s5(4)]. This must be made in writing and must be dated and signed, or signed at the direction

of the person making the appointment and witnessed by two
people [s5(5)]. There is no need for this document to be drawn
up by a lawyer or to form part of a will, though it can be. This
revokes all earlier appointments, unless it is clear that an
additional appointment is being made.

The guardianship comes into force (i.e. the guardian will acquire
parental responsibility for the child) [s5(6)] when the person who
made the appointment dies, under any of the following
circumstances [s5(7)]:

- if the child's other parent with parental responsibility dies at
  the same time, or is already dead;
- on the death of the child's other parent with parental
  responsibility;
- if the person making the appointment had, immediately prior
  to death, a Residence Order in effect with respect to the
  child, and the child's other parent did not.

Guardians can also be appointed by a court, either on application
or by their own motion in any family proceedings, where the
child has no living parent with parental responsibility or where a
parent holding a sole Residence Order in relation to a child has
died. The guardianship can be brought to an end by the court on
its own initiative in any family proceedings, on application by
any person with parental responsibility for the child, or (with the
leave of the court) by the child him or herself [s6(7)].

Adoption
Adoption law has been relatively unchanged by the Children Act
and currently is specified by the Adoption Act 1976 (as amended
by the Children Act 1989). However, adoption law is currently
under review at the time of writing. Adoption is dealt with in a
little more detail in chapter 8.

Acquisition of parental responsibility by local authorities

Local authorities gain strictly limited parental authority when
they are awarded an Emergency Protection Order (see
chapter 5). This offers them only the authority to take such

action as is reasonably required to safeguard or promote the child's welfare [s44(5)(b)]. They gain more extensive parental responsibility under a Care Order [s33(3)(a)] or an Order Freeing the Child For Adoption [Sched 10, para 6], to the extent that they gain the general authority to determine a child's upbringing (see chapter 8 for more details).

RESOLVING DISPUTES ABOUT A CHILD'S UPBRINGING

The Children Act was designed to bring about a number of improvements to the way disputes about children's upbringing are resolved. This applies when the child's parents divorce or separate, and in a variety of other situations.

Section 8 orders

The Children Act introduced four new orders, 'section 8 orders' (called this as they are contained in section 8 of the Act), which are intended to be used to resolve specific aspects of a child's care or upbringing. They are:

Residence Order: for settling the arrangements about the person(s) with whom a child is to live.

Contact Order: requires the person with whom a child lives (or is to live) to allow the child to visit or stay with the person named in the order, or for that person and the child otherwise to have contact (e.g. letters and telephone calls) with each other.

Prohibited Steps Order: used to prevent a step, which could be taken by a parent in meeting his or her responsibility from being taken by any person without the consent of the court (for example, to stop a parent from changing the child's school).

Specific Issue Order: directs that parental responsibility is exercised in a particular way (e.g. that a child will receive certain medical treatment).

These four orders are designed to provide a flexible, comprehensive and practical system for resolving disputes in a wide range of circumstances, in both 'private' and 'public' law. It is helpful to divide these into two kinds: Residence and Contact Orders; and Prohibited Steps and Specific Issue Orders.

Residence and Contact Orders

The most usual purpose of these two orders is to adjudicate between parents who, following divorce or separation, are unable to reach agreement about major matters to do with their children's upbringing. However, as we have seen already, they can also be used in other situations. For example, grandparents can apply for a Contact Order to allow them to see their grandchildren, and a step-parent can apply for a Residence Order in order to acquire parental responsibility.

Prohibited Steps and Specific Issue Orders

These orders provide all three levels of courts which make decisions about children's welfare and upbringing with the kinds of powers which formerly could only be exercised by the High Court (usually by way of wardship). For example, a hospital can apply for a Specific Issue Order to authorise a blood-transfusion for a child, where the parents have refused their consent; a young woman can apply for a Prohibited Steps Order to prevent her parents taking her away from the school she is attending. Separated parents can use them in similar ways if they are unable to resolve a dispute (e.g. about a child's religious worship).

Making section 8 orders

An application for a section 8 order can be made to any of the three levels of court. Courts can also make section 8 orders without any application having been made, in the course of other proceedings (either instead of or in addition to the order applied for) including:

- applications in connection with parental responsibility;
- divorce, nullity and separation proceedings;
- applications under domestic violence legislation;
- adoption proceedings;
- care proceedings;
- other proceedings under the High Court's inherent jurisdiction.

Usually, a section 8 order is heard with 14 days' notice having been served on the parties. However, all section 8 orders can, in certain circumstances, be applied for *ex parte* (i.e. on an emergency basis without the other side being given notice) with the leave of the Justices' Clerk (this is not required if the *ex parte* application is to the County or High Court). They must serve the order on each respondent (i.e. all those entitled to notice) within 48 hours of it being made.

The court may decide to make no order at all (indeed, it is required not to make one unless doing so is better for the child than making no order at all). It may make the order applied for, or it can make another order. For example, a mother might seek a Specific Issue Order to allow her to take her children abroad to live and the court might, having considered all the information in relation to the welfare checklist, decide to make a Residence Order in favour of the children's father.

Residence Order

A Residence Order specifies with whom the child is to live and gives the person in favour of whom it is made parental responsibility for the child, if they do not already have it. It also gives this person a number of other powers, including the authority to take the child out of the UK for up to a month (note the provisions of the Child Abduction Act 1984, discussed later in this chapter). If only one parent has a Residence Order with respect to a child and that parent appoints a guardian, then, on the death of that parent, the guardian will acquire parental responsibility for the child. A Residence Order also prevents the other parent exercising parental responsibility in a way that would undermine it (i.e. taking the child to live with them).

RESIDENCE ORDER [s8]

Who may apply? The child's parents and others (see Box 3.2) are entitled to apply. Any other person, including the child, may apply with leave of the court. The local authority is specifically prohibited from applying.

The court can also make the order on its own motion in any family proceedings.

Period of notice: fourteen days. In an emergency, an application can be made ex *parte*.

Parties: includes all those whom the applicant believes to have parental responsibility for the child.

Others entitled to notice: includes a person with whom the child is living, and the local authority if providing accommodation for the child.

Welfare principle: The welfare checklist applies, as do the presumption of no order [s1(5)] and paramountcy principle [s1(1)].

Powers and duties: The order will specify with whom the child shall live, and automatically gives the person in whose favour it is made parental responsibility for the child [s12].

In making the order, the court can give directions about how the order is to be carried out; impose conditions which must be complied with; direct that it have effect for a specified period; and make 'such incidental, supplemental or consequential provision as the court thinks fit' [s11(7)].

When the order is in force, no person may change the child's surname without the written consent of every person with parental responsibility or leave of the court. The child may not be removed from the UK without such written permission, except that the person holding the Residence Order may take the child outside the UK for a period of less than one month.

Duration: A Residence Order ceases to have effect if both parents, both having parental responsibility, live together for a continuous period exceeding six months, and when the child reaches the age of sixteen (eighteen in exceptional circumstances). The order is discharged by the making of a Care Order.

Challenge: Any person entitled to apply for a Residence Order can apply for its variation or discharge. Anyone else is entitled to do so if the order was made on their application. Appeal is to the High Court or Court of Appeal.

Under transitional arrangements, where a parent was granted custody of a child prior to the Children Act, they still have custody until a section 8 application is made under the Children Act 1989. The Residence Order is the only section 8 order which can be sought with respect to a child who is in the care of the local authority, although the local authority cannot itself apply for one. Its effect is to terminate the Care Order. Where a Residence Order is made in care or supervision proceedings (e.g. to enable the child to live with relatives), the court will usually accompany it with a Supervision Order (see chapter 8).

Enforcement
The Act contains specific provisions for the enforcement of a Residence Order [s14]. When one is in force and another person (including one in whose favour the order is also in force) breaches the arrangements made by the order, the holder of the Residence Order can seek its enforcement. Once the holder has served the order on the other person, he or she can require the other person to produce the child. If this person wilfully fails to comply, the holder of the Residence Order can apply to the Magistrates' Court (under section 63(3) of the Magistrates' Courts Act 1980) for enforcement, which can include a fine or imprisonment.

Contact Order

Case law in the 1970s established that contact (then termed access) was properly seen as a right of the child. The recent trend in case law is to assume that continued contact with both parents is usually beneficial for the child. Nonetheless, the courts also insist that each case must be decided on the basis of its own circumstances. It is clear (as a matter of practical reality as well as law) that a child who is capable of making an informed decision and does not want to have contact with a parent will not be forced to do so.

CONTACT ORDER [s8]

Who may apply? The child's parents, guardian and others (e.g. a person with whom the child has lived for three years) or any holder of a Residence Order are entitled to apply. Any other person, including the child, may apply with leave of the court. Foster-parents have to gain permission to apply from the local authority, unless they are a relative or have had the child living with them for more than three years.

A local authority cannot apply. This order cannot be made in relation to a child who is in local authority care – in this instance a Section 34 Contact Order must be applied for.

The court can also make the order on its own motion in any family proceedings.

Period of notice: fourteen days. In an emergency, an application can be made ex *parte*.

Parties: includes all those whom the applicant believes to have parental responsibility for the child.

Others entitled to notice: includes a person with whom the child is living, and the local authority if providing accommodation for the child.

Welfare principle: The welfare checklist applies, as do the presumption of no order [s1(5)] and paramountcy principle [s1(1)].

Powers and duties: The order will specify with whom the child should have contact.

In making the order, the court can give directions about how the order is to be carried out; impose conditions which must be complied with; direct that it have effect for a specified period; and make 'make such incidental, supplemental or consequential provision as the court thinks fit' [s11(7)].

Duration: A Contact Order ceases to have effect if both parents live together for a continuous period exceeding six months, and when the child reaches the age of sixteen (eighteen in exceptional circumstances). The order is discharged by the making of a Care Order.

Challenge: Any person entitled to apply for a Contact Order can apply for its variation or discharge. Anyone else is entitled to do so if the order was made on their application or they are named in the order. Appeal is to the High Court or Court of Appeal.

The changes introduced by the Children Act 1989 do not, however, directly resolve the problems of the effective enforcement of orders, and this may raise particular problems over enforcing Contact Orders. Many parents are unwilling to co-operate with any order made by the court relating to the child's contact with the other parent – these disputes can be bitter and the problems identified in earlier case law may well continue. However, the court is given the power to attach conditions to a Contact Order, which may be used in an attempt to reassure a parent that, for example, contact will be supervised. In one recent case, the court made a Residence Order in favour of the father and a Contact Order in favour of the child's aunt, with the condition that she did not discuss religious or spiritual matters with the child.

Specific Issue Order

As its name suggests, this order is designed to resolve a particular issue in dispute, such as medical treatment or an aspect of the child's education.

*S*PECIFIC ISSUE ORDER [s8]

Who may apply? The child's parents, guardian or any holder of a Residence Order are entitled to apply. Any other person, including the child, may apply with leave of the court. This order cannot be made in relation to a child who is in local authority care.

The court can make the order on its own motion in any family proceedings.

Period of notice: fourteen days. In an emergency an application can be made *ex parte*

Parties: includes all those whom the applicant believes to have parental responsibility for the child.

Others entitled to notice: includes the person with whom the child is living, and the local authority if providing accommodation for the child.

Welfare principle: The welfare checklist applies, as do the presumption of no order [s1(5)] and paramountcy principle [s1(1)].

Powers and duties: The order enables the court to determine some aspect of the child's care or upbringing. To achieve this, the court can give directions about how the order is to be carried out; impose conditions which must be complied with; direct that it have effect for a specified period; and make 'such incidental, supplemental or consequential provision as the court thinks fit' [s11(7)].

Constraints: The court may not make a Specific Issue Order with a view to achieving a result that could be achieved by a Residence or Contact Order, or that in any way is denied to the High Court in the exercise of its inherent jurisdiction by s100(2) of the Act.

Duration: A Specific Issue Order is, by its nature, time limited, as it is used to bring about a particular outcome (e.g. that the child should receive medical treatment). No order can be made that is to have effect beyond the child's sixteenth birthday, unless the circumstances are exceptional.

Challenge: Any person entitled to apply for a section 8 order can apply for its variation or discharge. Anyone else is entitled to do so if the order was made on their application. Appeal is to the High Court or Court of Appeal.

– METZUKAH'S STORY –

Metzukah is eleven and she lives with her mother, following her parent's divorce. She sees her father, Fikrit, most weekends. Last week on a visit she told her father that her mother plans for her to attend a mixed comprehensive when she moves up next year.

Fikrit is a devout Muslim. He is very unhappy about this plan for his daughter. He wants Metzukah to attend a private girl's school, which is run in accordance with his beliefs. He thought that was what Metzukah's mother wanted too, but every attempt he has made to discuss it has been met, he says, with a complete refusal to even consider his wishes.

He and his family are very upset. They are very worried about Metzukah's marriage prospects if she is not brought up correctly. Family honour is also an important consideration. Fikrit applies to the court for a Specific Issue Order, asking for directions that she will attend the school he believes is best for her.

As with all section 8 order applications, Fikrit's will be considered by the court in relation to the welfare checklist (see chapter 2). It is in a case like this that we can see just how complex and problematic the decisions will be – where there are completely divergent views about the child's needs and how best her welfare will be served. From Fikrit's perspective, for Metzukah to acquire Western values is to make her vulnerable, as a woman, to all the ills that Western culture brings – promiscuity, divorce and single parenthood. Most importantly she will also lose her ties with her wider family and religious community and, consequently, her status and honour within that community. Metzukah's mother, on the other hand, may feel that a strict Muslim education would be overly restrictive for her daughter.

The problem, for the court, will be in deciding between these two completely contrasting views, most probably with little knowledge and understanding themselves of the Muslim faith. The court could make no order at all. It could make the Specific Issue Order in Fikrit's favour, or a Residence Order in the mother's favour and a Contact Order directing that Metzukah is allowed to spend significant periods of time with her father and his extended family. The court is likely to seek a welfare report. The court welfare officer is required to ascertain Metzukah's wishes and feelings on the matter, and the court must take these into account.

Prohibited Steps Order

This order is aimed at restricting the way somebody (parents and others) can exercise parental responsibility. For example, it can be used to prevent a child being removed from the home where he or she is living, pending the outcome of proceedings as to where the child should live. Such an order cannot be used to prevent contact between parents, as this is not an aspect of parental responsibility.

P ROHIBITED STEPS ORDER [s8]

Who may apply? The child's parents, guardian or any holder of a Residence Order are entitled to apply. Any other person, including the child, may apply with leave of the court. This order cannot be made in relation to a child who is in local authority care.

The court can make the order on its own motion in any family proceedings.

Period of notice: fourteen days. In an emergency an application can be made *ex parte*.

Parties: includes all those whom the applicant believes to have parental responsibility for the child.

Others entitled to notice: includes the person with whom the child is living, and the local authority if providing accommodation for the child.

Welfare principle: The welfare checklist applies, as do the presumption of no order [s1(5)] and paramountcy principle [s1(1)].

Powers and duties: The order enables the court to prohibit the exercise of parental responsibility with respect to a particular form of action. To achieve this, the court can give directions about how the order is to be carried out; impose conditions which must be complied with; direct that it have effect for a specified period; and make 'such incidental, supplemental or consequential provision as the court thinks fit' [s11(7)].

Constraints: The court may not make a Prohibited Steps Order with a view to achieving a result that could be achieved by a Residence or Contact Order, or that in any way is denied to the High Court in the exercise of its inherent jurisdiction by s100(2) of the Act.

Duration: A Prohibited Steps Order is, by its nature, time limited, as it is used to bring about a particular outcome (e.g. that the child should not receive medical treatment). No order can be made that is to have effect beyond the child's sixteenth birthday, unless the circumstances are exceptional.

Challenge: Any person entitled to apply for a section 8 order can apply for its variation or discharge. Anyone else is entitled to do so if the order was made on their application. Appeal is to the High Court or Court of Appeal.

WHAT HAPPENS WHEN PARENTS SEPARATE?

The expectation is that no order will be made following parental separation or divorce. Usually what will happen is that the divorce petition will be accompanied by a *Statement of Arrangements for Children*, in which the petitioning parent gives details of the relevant 'children of the family', their circumstances and any proposal for change. This form is served on the respondent spouse, who is given the opportunity to submit a written reply. This, together with the original form, is considered by the judge before the granting of a decree. Where parents are in agreement, the judge will usually accept the arrangements they have made, although he or she can seek further information (including a welfare report), make a section 8 order or a Family Assistance Order (discussed later).

When the parents are married

If a married couple divorce, the question as to what will happen to their children is seen as a private concern, to be decided by them. Only if they cannot agree post-divorce arrangements for their children will the legal system be involved, and, even then, it will only be in exceptional circumstances that a full divorce decree will be delayed because of concerns over the children.

The aim is to encourage the parents to make their own decisions about their children. Given that the divorce court cannot take their parental responsibility away from them, it is intended that there will be nothing for the parents to fight over: there will no longer be 'winners' and 'losers'. All the divorce court can do is settle practical matters relating to the child's residence and contact. The legal system is expected to provide support in the form of conciliation services to encourage agreement.

It is now possible under the Children Act 1989 to get a joint Residence Order [s11(4)]. Previously, the idea that the child could live in two households was disapproved of by the courts, who placed emphasis on the stability arising out of having one home. Now the Act gives the court the power to 'specify the periods during which the child is to live in the different households concerned'. Of course, there is nothing preventing couples coming to a similar arrangement by agreement, thereby avoiding the necessity of a court hearing.

If the parents cannot agree on where the child should live and the contact arrangements, then they can apply to the court to settle their dispute. The section 1 principles apply in any section 8 order application and, if the application is contested, the court is under a duty to consider the welfare checklist. The child's welfare will be the court's paramount consideration and the court will have regard to the 'minimum intervention' principle contained in section 1(5) of the Children Act 1989. The Court Welfare Service, both in its role as conciliator and with respect to its responsibility to prepare welfare reports for the courts, will continue to play an important role in the context of divorce.

Despite the commitment to minimal intervention, it is recognised that, in some circumstances, the situation in which the divorce takes place is so problematic that direct intervention is needed. In such cases, the court can make a Family Assistance Order in addition to or instead of making any of the section 8 orders.

Family Assistance Order

The Family Assistance Order can be made in any family proceedings where the court is able to make a section 8 order. Unlike a section 8 order, however, the court makes it of its own motion (i.e. it cannot be applied for). The aim of the order is 'to provide short-term help to a family, to overcome problems and conflicts associated with their separation or divorce. Help may well be focused more on the adults than the child' [Guidance, Vol 1, para 2.50]. If the situation is more serious and the threshold criteria are satisfied, then a Supervision Order will be more appropriate (see chapter 8).

AMILY ASSISTANCE ORDER [s16]

Who may apply? Not applicable. Only the court on its own motion can make the order.

Welfare checklist: does not apply, but the presumption of no order [s1(5)] and paramountcy principle [s1(1)] do.

Grounds: The court can only make the order if:

- it has the power to make a section 8 order (though it does not have to make such an order); *and*
- the circumstances of the case are exceptional; *and*
- it has obtained the consent of every person named in the order, other than the child [s16(3)].

Powers and duties: The order requires either a probation officer or an officer of the local authority to be available to 'advise, assist and (where appropriate) befriend any person named in the order' [s16(10)]. The persons who can be named in the order are:

- any parent or guardian of the child;
- any person with whom the child is living or in whose favour a Contact Order is in force with respect to the child;
- the child.

Any person named in the order can be required to take such steps as may be specified to keep the officer informed of the address of any person named and to allow the officer to visit such person(s).

Duration: The order lasts a maximum of six months, although a new order can be made at the end of this period.

Challenge: Where a section 8 order is also in force with respect to the child, the officer can refer back to the court issues relating to the discharge or variation of the section 8 order during the period of a Family Assistance Order [s16(6)].

The effect of a Family Assistance Order is that a social worker or probation officer will be allocated to counsel family members and mediate between them. For example, they may work with the parents to set up and monitor arrangements for contact, where there is strong antagonism from one parent about allowing the other parent to have any contact at all. If the professional involved with the family is concerned about the welfare of the child, they can refer the case to the local authority for investigation.

— KATE AND JOE'S STORY —

Kate is six and Joe is three. Their mother, Alice, left their father, Julian, following a massive row in which he was very violent towards her. Alice has, since the divorce, been adamant that Julian should not know where they are living, as she fears he will be violent towards her again.

Subsequently, Alice has accused Julian of sexually abusing Kate. The local authority and police have investigated these allegations, including interviewing both of the children. They have found no firm evidence of sexual abuse, but remain somewhat concerned.

A Family Assistance Order has been made by the court, and a social worker has been working with Alice and Julian and providing supervision for Julian's contact with the children. When the six months comes to an end, the social worker recommends to the court that the Contact Order in Julian's favour directs that he may only see the children at his own parent's house. While the social worker regards the allegations of sexual abuse as most likely to be unfounded, she has observed that Kate is not very comfortable with her father, and Kate says she does not want to go to stay with him. The social worker believes that supervised contact is the safest plan and is most likely to work. Alice has grudgingly accepted this, but made it clear that she would 'do a moonlight' if unsupervised contact were ordered by the court.

Investigating concerns about the children

Where there are serious concerns about the children, the court has the power in divorce proceedings to require the local authority to investigate the child's circumstances. This is most likely to come about as the result of a report by the Court Welfare Service. If the court does direct the local authority to investigate the child's circumstances, then the local authority has to consider whether they should apply for a Care or Supervision Order; provide services or assistance for the child or family; or take any other action with respect to the child [s37(2)].

After undertaking such an investigation, the local authority is under a duty to provide the court with certain information and to comply with the request within a period of eight weeks unless the court otherwise directs [s37(3)&(4)]. In the meantime the court can make an Interim Care or Supervision Order as long as the court is satisfied that there are reasonable grounds for believing that the 'threshold criteria' are satisfied [s38(1)(b)&(2)]. (See chapter 8 for more details).

When the parents are not married

When the parents are not married to each other, what happens on separation will depend whether or not the father has acquired parental responsibility for the child.

When the father has parental responsibility

If the father has parental responsibility then, in the absence of any application by the mother or the child (who will require the leave of the court), he will retain it. The assumption will be, just as with divorcing married parents, that the parents will come to their own arrangements. However, unlike the divorce situation, there is no direct mechanism by which the legal system can intervene if there are concerns about the child's welfare. During divorce, the Court Welfare Service will identify those couples where they have concerns about a child and provide conciliation. In the event of a failure to come to an agreement, they will prepare a report for the court. By contrast, when unmarried parents separate, it will be up to the parents themselves to decide how they are going to arrange their parental responsibilities in the future, outside of any legal setting. If they cannot agree then, as in divorce, they can apply for a section 8 order and the court will decide the matter.

When the father does not have parental responsibility

As we have seen already in this chapter, while the term 'parent' in the Children Act 1989 includes the unmarried father, if he does not have parental responsibility and does not take steps to acquire it, there are important consequences:

1 He cannot prevent the removal of the child from the court's jurisdiction (i.e. taking the child out of the country) simply by refusing his consent. To do so he would have to apply for a Prohibited Steps Order.
2 His consent will not be needed for an adoption. If he wishes to prevent this happening he will need to apply for a Residence Order or a Parental Responsibility Order, in which case the application will be heard along with the adoption application.
3 He will be unable to object to the provision of accommodation for his child by the local authority or remove the child from such accommodation (see chapter 4).
4 If his child is in local authority care, he will be unable to apply for the discharge of the Care Order, although he will be able to apply for a Residence Order which, if made in his

favour, would have the effect of discharging the Care Order and giving him parental responsibility for his child.

If the father, instead, decides to apply for a Residence Order and the proceedings are contested, then the court will be required to consider the items in the welfare checklist. If successful, not only will the child come to live with him, but he will also acquire parental responsibility for the child which cannot be brought to an end prior to the expiry of the Residence Order. If, however, the unmarried father only wants to ensure his child will have contact with him, then he can apply for a Contact Order. Again, the court will be under a duty to have regard to the welfare checklist.

Whatever the father decides to do, each case will be decided on its own unique set of circumstances and each application must be considered separately (i.e. brothers and sisters should not be dealt with together). In any such contested proceedings, the court has the powers to direct that an investigation is made into the child's circumstances [s37]; to make an order which contains directions and imposes conditions; or to make another order entirely (e.g. a Contact Order).

Post-separation disputes

In practice, the powers of the court under the Children Act 1989 to resolve disputes (over children) between couples are the same irrespective of whether the dispute arises during their relationship, at the time of their separation or afterwards. Applications for section 8 orders can be made by any parent at any time up until the child's sixteenth birthday, unless there are exceptional circumstances – in which case the order can last until the child's eighteenth birthday.

– MOLLIE'S STORY –

When Mollie's parents divorced, after an initial period of antagonism they were able to come to an amicable agreement by which Mollie lived with her mother and spent one weekend a month with her father, as well as longer periods in holiday times.

Mollie's father re-married fairly soon and Mollie seemed to settle well with having a new step-mother. However, after five years Mollie's mother became ill and she could not care for Mollie any longer. Mollie went to live with her father and his wife. It soon became clear that Mollie's mother was unlikely to recover. Mollie's father and his wife decided to apply for a Residence Order so that her step-mother would have parental responsibility for Mollie.

In a situation like this the court is likely to make the order, to provide Mollie with a secure future. It could, if it thought it necessary, also make a Contact Order in her mother's favour, though she will continue to have parental responsibility for Mollie.

Vexatious litigants

There is provision for a situation where there is a protracted dispute. Where one parent is unwilling to accept the court's decision and makes repeated applications for variation and new section 8 applications (in legal terminology a 'vexatious litigant'), the courts have the power to prohibit further applications, save with the court's leave [s91(14)].

Other agencies involved with the children of separating parents

Where separating parents (irrespective of whether they were married or not) agree to continue to share responsibility for the upbringing of their children and strive to do so in an amicable fashion, there will be little cause for anybody else to get involved. However, where conflicts arise and where, in particular, these are resolved by legal intervention, it will be important for those agencies involved with the child(ren) to know where they stand, and to have developed procedures for conforming to the court orders that have been made.

Where contact is prohibited between a child and one parent.

This is likely to arise only where there are serious concerns about the child's safety while in the care of the parent whose contact is prohibited. For example, this is a situation which may ensue from a criminal prosecution of the parent for an offence against the child or another child in the family.

In this situation, if the parent who has care of the child makes use of day-care or child-minding services (or, indeed, others such as sporting and leisure facilities), then he or she will need to inform whoever is in charge of these facilities. Managers of such facilities will need to keep records of who is entitled to collect the child. They will also need to have a system to make sure that all staff fully understand what action they must take to protect the child if the other parent turns up on the premises. This situation is examined in more detail in chapter 6.

Contact Order with conditions attached.
This is the kind of situation which may arise because of lesser concerns for the child's safety (for example, where there are unproven allegations of abuse) or where there is a fear that the child may be taken away or abducted.

Where the Contact Order lays down conditions about contact between the child and the named parent, specifying the time, place and conditions (for example, that it must be supervised) under which it must take place, then staff working at day-care centres, child-minders and others (for example, friends with whom the child stays) will need to be informed by the parent who has care of the child about what action to take in the event of the other parent turning up in contravention of the conditions laid down by the court. The local authority's liaison with the education service should result in schools also being informed of who, for example, is now able to collect the child from school.

Residence Order with conditions attached
The kind of situation where this would arise is where, for example, the parent with the Residence Order is directed to allow the child to attend religious instruction, even though this is contrary to their own beliefs. Here the situation is more difficult since it is quite possible that service providers (for example, day care and schools) will not find out about the conditions unless the parent tells them. In such cases, it will be up to the other

parent, on having the order made, to make sure that all those who may be involved in meeting its directions know where they stand and what is expected of them.

Children in need

The aftermath of relationship breakdown often leads to severe financial hardship and can leave the parent with care with insufficient support to look after his or her child. This may, in some cases, lead to the child being 'in need' (under the provisions of the Children Act). If this is the case, then the local authority will have a wide range of duties towards such children and the family they are living with – these are discussed further in chapter 4.

FINANCIAL PROVISION FOR CHILDREN

The Children Act 1989 allows parents, irrespective of whether they are married or not, to apply for financial relief for their children. The courts have wide powers to make financial orders for the benefit of children, although the Magistrates' Court has more limited powers than the County Court or High Court. However, these powers are largely superseded by the operation of the Child Support Act 1991, which came into force in April 1993. (The Act will be fully operational by 1997). The net effect of the Child Support Act 1991 is that it is the Child Support Agency, not the courts, who will be responsible for the assessment, collection and enforcement of maintenance payments. The Act introduces a number of formulae which are used to calculate the 'maintenance assessment'. In other words, the Child Support Agency will calculate the correct amount of maintenance in a case, whereas in the past it was a matter of the discretion of the court.

The courts will, however, continue to be responsible for applications for lump sum provision and property transfer orders for the benefit of children. In addition, they will have a residual role in relation to awards for topping up a maintenance assessment already in force, disabled children, school fees and step-children.

CHALLENGES BY CHILDREN AND YOUNG PEOPLE ABOUT THEIR UPBRINGING

One of the important provisions of the Act is that which allows a child to apply (with leave) to the court for a section 8 order – the so-called 'child divorces parents' cases of the media headlines.

The Children Act 1989 states that, where the applicant for a section 8 order is a child, 'the court may only grant leave if it is satisfied that he has sufficient understanding to make the proposed application' [s10(8)]. This is an important filter mechanism, which should reassure those who worry that the law may have gone too far down the road of children's rights in allowing children to apply, for example, for a Residence Order to allow him or her to leave home and go to live somewhere else. Courts are not known for their radicalism and it is absurd to think that – as some journalists have suggested – courts will countenance allowing a child to apply for an order, simply because he or she has got into a row over bedtimes or pocket money. Courts will want to be convinced that a child has a sensible and serious reason for making an application.

What the Children Act has done is to provide children with an avenue whereby they can initiate action to resolve an aspect of their upbringing which *they* perceive as crucial to their welfare. Even if the court grants leave to apply, at any subsequent hearing the court will be obliged to consider the paramountcy principle and the 'no order' requirement [s1], and to examine the application with respect to the welfare checklist. Thus a so-called 'divorce' will only be granted in circumstances where the child can show that a move is warranted and offers a significantly better environment in which they will be cared for. Note too that the notion of 'divorce' is not appropriate, as the child's parent(s) will still have parental responsibility (though it will be shared and may be constrained). They will continue to be, for example, consulted about the child's upbringing and will expect to have contact with the child except where this is specifically prohibited.

Finally, in any section 8 proceedings (as they are family proceedings) the court has the power to direct the local authority to undertake an investigation of the child's circumstances. So, the ability of children to raise matters regarding their upbringing before a court may well be critical in alerting the local authority, and others, as to the serious dilemmas confronting the child (e.g. undetected abuse by a parent or step-parent).

CHILD ABDUCTION

Abduction of children following relationship breakdown is still rare, but the distress caused to parents and children can be great. In 1991 the Lord Chancellor's Department estimated that there were over 200 abductions abroad – other estimates are much higher.

BOX 3.3   THE CHILD ABDUCTION ACT 1984

The Child Abduction Act 1984 creates two criminal offences, one concerning abduction by a person 'connected with the child' and one by an unconnected person.

When a person *connected with the child* takes or sends a child under the age of 16 out of the UK without the appropriate consent, that person is guilty of an offence. A person who is connected with a child includes the child's parent (including an unmarried father), guardian, the holder of a Residence Order in relation to the child, or any person who has custody of the child.

The appropriate consent means *either* the consent of *each* of the following:

- the child's mother;
- the child's father if he has parental responsibility for the child;
- any guardian of the child;
- any person in whose favour a Residence Order is in force, with respect to the child;
- any person who has custody of the child;

or

- the permission of the court.

There are three defences to this offence under the Child Abduction Act 1984:

1 The alleged abductor believed that the person consented or would consent if they knew all the circumstances.
2 The alleged abductor had taken all reasonable steps to communicate with the other person, but had been unable to do so.
3 The required consent had been unreasonably refused.

When a person *unconnected with the child*, without lawful authority or reasonable excuse, takes or detains a child under the age of 16 so as to remove him or her from the control of any person who has lawful control of the child, or so as to keep him or her out of the lawful control of any person entitled to such control (e.g. both the child's parents), then that person is guilty of an offence.

There are two defences to this offence. First, if the alleged abductor believed that the child was aged sixteen or older. Second, in the case of a child of unmarried parents, if the alleged abductor had reasonable grounds for believing he was the child's father.

Making something a criminal offence does not stop it happening! However, there are a number of ways that a parent who is concerned about the possibility of abduction can reduce its likelihood.

Strategies for preventing child abduction

Precautionary steps to prevent abduction involve avoiding (as far as this is possible) situations where it is made possible. For example, a parent can inform the child's nursery or school that the child should not be handed over to anyone other than people he or she specifies. If both parents have parental responsibility for the child, then, if abduction is feared, contact arrangements should be made in ways which ensure supervision (e.g. at the home of a relative). For example, an application for a Contact Order can be made, setting out the concerns about abduction, providing information that this may be a possibility and seeking a direction that contact should be appropriately supervised.

If the child has his or her own passport, it should be kept in a safe place. Similarly, other key documents (such as the child's birth certificate and NHS card) should be kept safely. If the child does not have a passport, an objection can be lodged in writing at the Passport Office, stating that the child may not be included on the other parent's passport. The Passport Office will comply with this request as long as there is a court order which:

1   gives custody or a Residence Order to the objector;
2   prohibits the removal of the child from the UK;
3   contains a direction regarding the obtaining or holding of a passport.

It is also prudent to keep a record of the likely abductor's passport number, in case it proves necessary to prevent an attempted abduction. If the possibility of abduction is feared, there should be an application for a Residence Order with these directions included (see Box 3.4).

Prohibited Steps Order

Where there are real concerns about an imminent abduction, a parent can apply for a Prohibited Steps Order, either to prevent any further contact between the child and a named person or to stop the child being taken out of the country by the named person. In considering whether to make the order, the court will only be concerned with what is best for the child (not the rights and wrongs as between the adults in dispute) and will be guided by the welfare checklist. It follows that, with reference to an older child, what he or she says will have a bearing on the decision of the court. This application can be *ex parte*.

An injunction

Two situations in which an injunction to prevent abduction can be obtained are:

1   while applying for a Residence Order;
2   while applying for wardship.

A Residence Order can be applied for on an emergency basis where the circumstances are exceptional. In this case, the application is *ex parte* (i.e. without the other side being given notice of the proceedings). At the same time as making the order, the County or High Court could grant an injunction prohibiting the removal of the child from the jurisdiction. Again, in making any decision, the court will be concerned only with the welfare of the child.

Given that the Children Act 1989 provides effective remedies it is unlikely that use of the wardship jurisdiction will be common (if for no other reason than parents are unlikely to get legal aid for such proceedings). However, where the child concerned is over sixteen or there is a real and immediate threat of abduction, wardship may be the most appropriate remedy. One advantage is that, as soon as the child is warded, the child automatically cannot be taken out of the jurisdiction.

In addition, it is possible for the court to order that a person enter into a bond for a sum of money, which will be forfeited if he or she fails to comply with the order of the court. Even though this requires his or her consent, it can still be of practical value (e.g. it can be set as a condition for allowing the child to be taken abroad, to help ensure that the child is returned).

Criminal proceedings

Under the Child Abduction Act 1984, the police can arrest anyone whom they reasonably suspect of attempting to take a child out of the country without permission, and can operate a 'port alert' system whereby immigration officials at ports and airports will be informed and the child's name put on a 'stop list'. Once the child's name is on the 'stop list', it will remain there for four weeks.

BOX 3.4	WHAT TO DO IF IT IS FEARED THE CHILD MAY BE BEING ABDUCTED

If is it is feared a child is being abducted, the police should be informed immediately. The following information should be provided to assist the police/immigration officials in their task:

- the child's name, sex, date of birth, description, nationality and passport number;
- the name and description of the person likely to remove the child, in addition to their nationality and passport number;
- your name, relationship to the child, nationality, and your solicitor's telephone number;
- the likely destination, time of travel and port(s) of embarkation;
- the reasons for the port alert;
- the details of the person to whom the child should be returned if detained.

While the port alert procedure is an important mechanism for preventing child abduction, the numbers of children travelling abroad is so large that the prevention of unauthorised removal cannot be guaranteed.

Civil law remedies

Under the Family Law Act 1986, certain orders relating to children made in one part of the UK can be enforced in another part. Section 33 of the Act enables a court, in certain proceedings, to order a person to disclose relevant information. If a person is so ordered, they must comply. Any statement made in compliance with such an order will only be admissible in proceedings for perjury (giving priority to finding out where the child is rather than punishing an abductor and any accomplices). In addition, section 34 of the Act provides that, where a person is required by a section 8 order to give up a child to another person and refuses to do so, the court may make an order authorising an officer of the court or a police constable to take charge of the child and deliver the child to the other person.

International legal framework

The Child Abduction and Custody Act 1985 gives effect to two international conventions: the *Hague Convention on the Civil Aspects of International Child Abduction,* and the *European Convention on Recognition and Enforcement of Decisions Concerning Custody of Children.* Their purpose is to secure the quick return of children to the country in which they have their home. One drawback with these conventions is that so few countries have signed them. What therefore appears to be, on paper, an effective mechanism for securing the return of abducted children is, in reality, much less so. This is why prevention is a better strategy than seeking a legal remedy once an abduction has been carried out. Further information can be obtained from the Lord Chancellor's Department and REUNITE (see addresses at the end of the book).

4 *Welfare services for children and their families*

In this chapter we outline the responsibilities that local authorities have to provide and regulate welfare services for children and their families, sometimes referred to as the Children Act's 'Part III provisions'. The Children Act 1989 also places some general duties on local authorities to provide services for all the children in their area and to offer a range of more comprehensive services for children who are identified as being 'in need'.

LOCAL AUTHORITY POWERS AND DUTIES TO PROVIDE SERVICES

While the bulk of their responsibilities are to children 'in need', the Children Act gives local authorities a number of powers and duties towards all the children living within their area, irrespective of whether they are 'in need' (see Box 4.1).

> **BOX 4.1** LOCAL AUTHORITY POWERS AND DUTIES TOWARDS ALL CHILDREN LIVING IN THEIR AREA

Powers
Local authorities have powers to provide:

1 day care for children aged five or under who are not yet attending school;

2 accommodation for children under the age of 16, with their parent's agreement, if this will safeguard or promote the child's welfare;

3   accommodation for young persons aged between 16 and 21, even without their parent's permission, if this will safeguard or promote the young person's welfare;

4   care or supervised activities outside school hours or during school holidays;

5   facilities (including training, advice, guidance and counselling) for those caring for or accompanying children in day care.

As powers, note that these are what local authorities *can* do, but are not obliged to do.

Duties

Local authorities do, however, have the following duties towards all the children who live in their area:

1   to take reasonable steps to reduce the need to bring care or supervision proceedings, or criminal proceedings, against children;

2   to take reasonable steps to avoid the need for children to be placed in secure accommodation;

3   to take reasonable steps, through the provision of services, to prevent children suffering ill-treatment or neglect;

4   to provide family centres as appropriate;

5   to publish information about its services and to take reasonable steps to ensure that those who might benefit from services receive the relevant information.

As duties, these are all things the local authority *must* do.

Local authority responsibilities to provide services for children in need

Each local authority is under a duty to 'take reasonable steps to identify the extent to which there are children in need within its area', to assess the needs of these children and then to plan service provision to meet them. Local authorities are required to publicise information about their services and to 'take such steps as are reasonably practicable to ensure that those who might benefit from the services receive the information relevant to them'.

BOX 4.2   CHILDREN IN NEED

Section 17(10) defines a child as 'in need' if:

1   the child is unlikely to achieve or maintain, or to have the opportunity of achieving or maintaining, a reasonable standard of health or development without the provision of services;

2   the child's health or development is likely to be significantly impaired, or further impaired, without the provision of such services; *or*

3   the child is disabled.

A child is defined as disabled if he or she is 'blind, deaf or dumb or suffers from mental disorder of any kind or is substantially and permanently handicapped by illness, injury or congenital deformity or such other disability as may be prescribed' [s17(11)].

Local authorities have an obligation to 'safeguard and promote the welfare of children within their area who are in need; and so far as is consistent with that duty, to promote the upbringing of such children by their families, by providing a range and level of services appropriate to those children's needs' [s17(1)].

The duties placed on local authorities towards children in need are contained in Part III of the Children Act 1989 and Part I Schedule 2 to the Act (see Box 4.3).

BOX 4.3   LOCAL AUTHORITY DUTIES TO CHILDREN IN NEED

Children living with their families

The local authority is under a statutory duty to provide services for children in need while they are living with their families, including:

- advice, guidance and counselling;
- occupational, social, cultural and recreational activities;
- home help (which may include laundry facilities);
- facilities for or assistance with travelling, to enable families to make use of these services;
- assistance to enable the child to have a holiday;
- family centres;
- appropriate day care for children who are aged five or under and not yet attending school;
- after-school care and care in school holidays, including supervised activities.

Accommodation as a service

In addition, local authorities must make available to children in need:

- accommodation (e.g. foster care) for children where they have no parent, are lost or abandoned, or where their parents cannot care for them;
- accommodation (e.g. a place in a hostel) for children aged 16 or over, even without their parent's permission, whose welfare is likely to be seriously prejudiced without it.

When children are accommodated, they are 'looked after' by the local authority, who then have further obligations towards them (see chapters 8 and 9).

Discretion

While these duties are qualified, they nonetheless represent the broad tenor of what is expected. Other services can be provided if they will help to safeguard or promote the child's welfare. All services must be offered without payment for families receiving income support or family credit. Other families may be required to contribute to the cost of services, if they have the means to do so.

These obligations place a considerable responsibility on local authorities, although they are given a degree of discretion in that they are only obliged by law to 'make such provision as they consider appropriate for... the services to be available', and they are only expected to provide those services which they have identified as required by the children in need living in their area. Guidance [Vol 2, para 11] states that:

> *Local authorities are not expected to meet every individual need, but they are asked to identify the extent of need and then make decisions on the priorities for service provision in their area in the context of that information and their statutory duties.*

What they are required to provide will therefore vary from one area to another. However, the Act makes it clear that not only is there a duty to provide a range of services, but that these services must reflect the racial, religious and linguistic backgrounds of the children concerned. In other words, in areas where there are significant numbers of families from ethnic minority cultures, the mix of services provided must address the needs of their children, including the need to feel that their cultural identity is respected and valued.

Local authorities do have considerable flexibility in the way they fulfil their obligations of service provision to children in need and their families. They can provide the service directly themselves; they can co-ordinate their work with other agencies; and they can facilitate the provision of services by others.

Purposes for which services are intended

Services for children in need are intended to offer positive support to families to help them to bring up their children themselves. The local authority is under a general duty:

- to safeguard and promote the welfare of children within its area who are in need; *and*
- so far as consistent with that duty, to promote the upbringing of such children by their families by providing a range and

level of services appropriate to those children's needs [s17(1)].

Services for disabled children have particular functions, which are:

- to minimise the effect on disabled children within their area of their disabilities;
- to give such children the opportunity to lead lives which are as normal as possible.

At the same time, the Act retains the notion of a preventive function. Local authorities are required to take reasonable steps designed to reduce the need to bring any proceedings which might lead to a child being taken into care, placed under a Supervision Order, or subject to criminal proceedings. The Act also seeks to prevent the removal of children by giving local authorities powers to assist an adult (e.g. an alleged abuser) to move out of the home rather than remove the child [Sched 2, para 5]. The authority may assist that other person to obtain alternative accommodation, including providing cash to pay for it.

REGULATING STANDARDS OF SERVICE

Not only must local authorities ensure that certain services are provided, they also have extensive powers and duties to regulate standards of service provision.

Day care

Day care is defined as looking after children under the age of eight for more than two hours in any day other than on domestic premises. The 'two hour rule' applies to the time that the person providing day care is available to look after children, rather than the time actually spent looking after an individual child.

Those providing group day-care or nursery facilities are required to *register* with the local authority. It is a criminal offence to fail to register without reasonable excuse. For their part, local authorities are required to keep a register of those providing day care for children and this register has to be accessible to the public. They are authorised to inspect and enter premises at any time, without a warrant, and must conduct an annual inspection of premises used for day care. A local authority can, in emergencies, apply to court *ex parte* for the cancellation of registration in order to protect children. The local authority is required to specify the number of persons required to assist in looking after children on the premises, and to direct the person registered to notify them of any change in the facilities provided and in the period during which they are provided. Failure to comply constitutes a criminal offence.

Even though registration relates to the *person* providing the day care rather than the premises on which it is provided, separate applications for registration must be submitted for different premises. Local authorities can charge a fee for the original application, as well as an annual fee to cover the costs of inspection. Local authorities must, in making any arrangements for the provision of day care within their area, have regard to the different racial groups to which children in need within their area belong [Sched 2, para 11(a)]. Where the families living in an area comprise a range of ethnic and racial backgrounds, day-care provision is expected to reflect this, so that children receive appropriate care.

Child-minding

Child-minding involves looking after children under the age of eight for reward – a nanny is exempt, as well as a parent, relative, person with parental responsibility or foster-parent. Similar registration and inspection duties apply to child-minding as to day care. When registering a person as a child-minder, the local authority is under a duty to impose such requirements on the applicant as are reasonable. The local authority must:

1 specify the maximum number of children;
2 require the premises and equipment used to be adequately maintained and kept safe;
3 require a record to be kept of the name and address of:

    (a) any child looked after,

    (b) any person who assists in looking after such a child, *and*

    (c) any person living or likely to be living on those premises;

4   require that they be notified by the child-minder, in writing, of any change among those persons looking after such children or living on the premises.

In addition to these, the local authority may impose and vary other requirements which are not incompatible with the above. Failure without reasonable excuse to comply with such requirements is a criminal offence.

Private fostering

Special arrangements are made in the Act to cover private fostering (section 67 and *Guidance and Regulations* Volume 8). These provide for registration and inspection of households where children are privately fostered, and intervention where there are concerns about the child's welfare.

Refusal of registration

The local authority may refuse to register an applicant if they consider the premises to be used for child-minding or day care are not fit for looking after children under eight. Similarly, they may refuse registration if they believe that any of the people employed, living, or looking after children on the premises is not fit to be in the proximity of children under eight. Certain people will be automatically disqualified from registration (e.g those convicted of specified offences).

Cancellation of registration

Local authorities may at any time cancel the registration of a person, if they consider that the circumstances of the case justify it or the care provided is seriously inadequate for the needs of the children concerned (including consideration of their religious persuasion, racial origin, and cultural and linguistic background).

They can also cancel a registration if the registered person has contravened or failed to comply with any requirement imposed, or failed to pay the annual fee within the prescribed time.

– MARCIA'S STORY –

Marcia is three. Her mother and father both work, and she is looked after during the day by Louise, who is a registered child-minder.

About six months ago, Louise's father came to live with her. Marcia got on with him well at first and enjoyed having another 'granpa'. They used to go to the park together and he read her stories. One day, however, Marcia came home in tears. She told her Mum that 'granpa Harry' had called her a 'dirty wog' and a 'nigger kid' and said other nasty things to her. Marcia's mother took this up with Louise, who said her father was only joking and, although she admitted he was rather racially prejudiced, he didn't mean any harm.

Marcia's mother was not satisfied and decided to take Marcia away and find another child-minder. She called up social services and made a complaint.

The local authority will have to take this seriously. They will need to visit Louise's home and talk with the father. If they view his behaviour as rendering Louise's care seriously inadequate, the local authority may decided to cancel Louise's registration. Guidance [Vol 2, para 6.10] states:

> *Children from a very young age learn about different races and cultures including religion and languages and will be capable of assigning different values to them. The same applies to gender and making distinctions between male and female roles. It is important that people working with young children are aware of this, so that their practice enables the children to develop positive attitudes to differences of race, culture, language and differences of gender.*

Thus having somebody in the home displaying racist attitudes cannot be simply tackled by placing only white children there. It is, in itself, a problem.

Appeals

The following decisions can be appealed against:

- a refusal of registration;
- cancellation of registration;
- a refusal of consent by virtue of being disqualified under Schedule 9, paragraph 2;
- the imposition, removal or variation of any requirement under section 72 or section 73;
- a refusal to grant any application for the variation or removal of any such requirement.

The appeals procedure includes a right to object to any of the above decisions before they are actually taken, as well as a right of appeal to the court afterwards. The steps are as follows:

1 The local authority must serve *notice* of its intention to take the step in question. This notice must include the reasons for the decision and inform the person concerned of his or her rights under the section.
2 The recipient has a right to object, which must be communicated in writing.
3 If the local authority decides, nevertheless, to take the step in question, it must send the person concerned a written notice of its decision.
4 At this stage, the person concerned can appeal to the court even if earlier he or she did not state an objection.

The court can, on allowing an appeal, impose requirements. It can also vary a requirement appealed against, rather than cancelling it.

Emergency action

The appeals procedure is lengthy and not suited to cases of emergency. Where it is believed that children are at immediate risk of significant harm, there is a special procedure whereby an application can be made to the court *ex parte* and supported by a written statement of the authority's reasons for making it. On such an application the court can make an order cancelling a person's registration, varying any requirement or removing an existing requirement, if it appears to the court that a child who is being or may be looked after by a child-minder or in day-care provision is suffering or likely to suffer significant harm.

Family centres

Unusually, family centres are specifically mentioned in the Act [Sched 2(9)] and their role in helping families is acknowledged. The Act describes the services that may be available at the family centre as:

- occupational, social, cultural or recreational activities;
- advice, guidance or counselling;
- the provision of accommodation.

Guidance identifies three main types of family centre [Vol 2, para 3.20]:

Therapeutic: skilled workers carry out intensive casework with families experiencing severe difficulties, with the aim of improving their ability to function as a family and the relationships between parents and children or between siblings.

Community: Local voluntary groups, including churches, may provide a neighbourhood-based facility for parents to use as a meeting place and to take part in particular activities.

Self-help: these may be run as a co-operative venture by a community group and are likely to offer various support services for families in an informal and unstructured way.

Accommodating children

Accommodating children is a service to be offered to children and their families. It is fundamentally different from the former (much criticised) system of 'voluntary care' and is more like forms of respite care offered to families with older relatives, which are intended to take the pressure off the family at times of crisis. Local authorities are required to provide accommodation for any child in need within their area where: there is no person who has parental responsibility for the child; the child is lost or has been abandoned; or the person who has been caring for the child is prevented from providing him or her with suitable accommodation, and it appears to the local authority that the child requires accommodation [s20(1)]. Local authorities are specifically prohibited from providing accommodation for a child if anybody with parental responsibility is willing and able to provide accommodation for the child or wants to make their own arrangements for the child to be accommodated. As a service, it can be terminated at will. Any person who has parental responsibility for the child may at any time remove the child.

– ICHIRIO'S STORY –

Ichirio is seven and is living in England with his mother and father as his parents are both working here. While his mother was away in Canada on an extended business trip, Ichirio's father was seriously injured in a car accident. The family have no relatives in the UK.

Contact was made by telephone with the child's mother, who asked for temporary foster-parents to be found to look after Ichirio until she could get back. On her return the next day, the mother decided that it would be best for Ichirio to stay with the foster-parents for a few days until she could make other arrangements, as she was spending most of her time at the hospital where her husband was seriously ill. Ichirio's mother agreed to pay for the foster care.

Three days later, Ichirio's grandmother arrived from Vancouver and, at his mother's request, Ichirio was immediately returned to live with her and the grandmother. Sadly, Ichirio's father died a few days later.

In looking for foster-parents for Ichirio, the local authority should – as far as possible – find out whether the child or his mother have any strong views as to what kind of people should look after the boy. They should try to find out whether they feel it is important for the foster-parents to practise their family's religion, or whether it matters more to make sure Ichirio can stay at the same school and be close to his friends. They should consult Ichirio's school and the family doctor. Although this placement turns out to be for only a few days, the local authority must still do their best to unsettle him as little as possible, especially at such a sad time.

We will look in more detail at the arrangements that must be made for children who are accommodated, and the powers and duties of local authorities towards children they are looking after (both accommodated children and those in care) in chapter 9, which considers children living away from home.

5 *Child protection*

In this chapter we will explore the specific measures in the Children Act for child protection and the arrangements made to co-ordinate work between agencies. We will examine how child abuse is investigated, and look at some of the dilemmas posed by the potential for parallel prosecution of those alleged to have assaulted the child.

LOCAL AUTHORITY DUTY TO INVESTIGATE

The Children Act [s47] places a duty on local authorities to investigate any concerns about a child's safety – when these are reported to them, when they become aware of them through their own casework with a family, and in circumstances where other professionals have intervened (e.g. where the child is taken into police protection, or where a child has persistently failed to comply with an Education Supervision Order).

This means that, whenever somebody passes on information to social services that suggests a child may be at risk of significant harm, they are obliged to follow up those concerns. Others (for example, other local authorities and education, housing and health departments) are required to assist the investigation by providing information (except 'where doing so would be unreasonable in all the circumstances of the case' [s47(10)]). Where access to the child is prevented (for example, where parents will not allow a social worker to see the child), then the Act provides ways of overcoming this – the Emergency Protection Order and police powers to intervene, which will be described later in this chapter.

If the local authority concludes, as a consequence of its investigations, that it should take action to safeguard or promote the child's welfare, it is expected to do this 'so far as it is both within its power and reasonably practicable to do so' [s47(8)]. The general principle is that, wherever possible, it should seek to 'safeguard or promote the child's welfare' by way of working with the family – identifying the child as 'in need' and providing appropriate services to address the problems the family is facing, so that the risk of ill-treatment to the child is removed and the child can achieve adequate standards of health and development. Only where this is not possible should it seek to intervene in a compulsory manner.

The investigation process

Before we look at the specific measures of the Children Act designed for compulsory intervention to protect a child, it is helpful to briefly review the usual course an investigation will take. This will help to put the law in the context of practice.

Often an investigation is conducted jointly by social services and the police, especially where sexual abuse is suspected. This is because, as well as seeking to discover whether the child has been or is at risk of 'significant harm', there may be the possibility of pursuing a criminal prosecution against the person(s) suspected of harming the child. Thus the investigative process often has two, not entirely compatible, functions:

1 to establish whether the child is being significantly harmed or is at risk of significant harm, and to devise a plan for protecting the child;
2 to establish whether a crime has been committed against the child, and to determine whether to pursue a prosecution against the alleged offender.

Most local authorities have set up joint police/social work child protection teams, with the purpose of co-ordinating these two activities and conducting them in parallel.

We can consider the investigative process as a series of stages (see Figure 5.1) although, in reality, these will seldom be discrete and

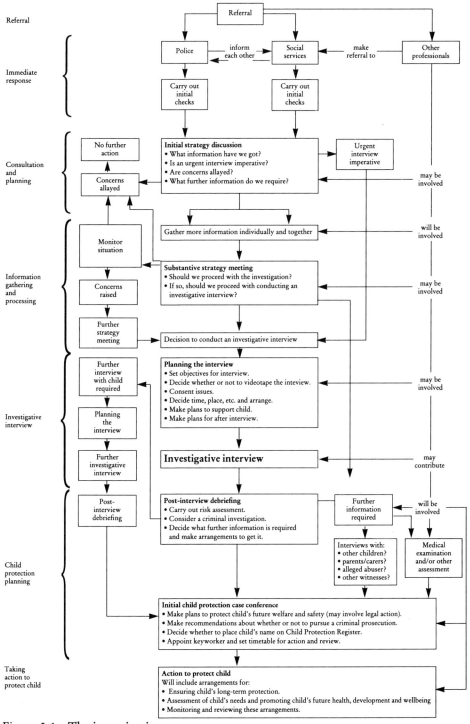

Figure 5.1 The investigative process

the actual process will be more complicated. Also, of course, it will vary considerably according to circumstances and the kinds of 'harm' suspected.

Referral

While a referral may come from many sources, it will lead to a statutory [s47] investigation once it is passed onto either the social services, the police or, in some circumstances, the NSPCC. The referral will usually be directed to a member of the child protection team, who will inform their counterpart in the other agency.

Immediate response

When the referral suggests that the child may be in immediate and serious danger, action can be taken straightaway. For example, the police may go to the child's home and take the child into police protection. However, in most cases there will be no such urgency and often the referral will take the form of vague suspicions or worries, with little concrete information to go on. In such situations, the course of investigation will depend upon the circumstances of the case. For example, where the concerns are about long-term neglect, such as a small baby who is failing to thrive, social services are likely to work closely with health professionals, with the police only getting involved if the situation suddenly deteriorates.

Where, however, there are suspicions that serious physical violence or sexual assault may be involved, the police and social services will usually work together. They will begin by each agency carrying out initial checks to get some baseline information. The social worker, for example, will consult the *Child Protection Register* (described later in this chapter) to see if the child (or another child in the family) has already been determined as 'at risk'. They will also consult the social service files, to see whether the family is already known to them. Checks may also be made with, for example, the family's health visitor, to find out if they have any relevant information. The police officer will check criminal records to discover whether any information is held on the person suspected of harming the child.

Initial consultation and planning

Once these initial checks have been carried out, staff from the police and social services child-protection teams will hold a strategy meeting. This may be a face-to-face meeting, but it will usually be a telephone call. The purpose of this discussion is to plan the investigation. At this stage the details of the case should not be discussed in any more detail than is necessary to decide how the investigation is to be pursued. Consideration must be given, however, to the urgency of the case.

In some situations the concerns raised by the referral can be fully allayed at this point and a decision made to take no further action. However, this would be unusual. In other situations, concerns will be so urgent and serious that immediate action will need to be taken (such as seeking an Emergency Protection Order). In most cases, however, this meeting/discussion will be used to decide what further information is required, how it is to be obtained and by whom. Plans will be made for a further strategy meeting once the information has been obtained. Occasionally, at this point, it will be decided to move straight to interviewing the child. This may be the case, for example, when a child expresses a wish to talk immediately about a sexual assault. Generally, though, this will be left until sufficient information has been gathered to indicate whether a formal interview with the child is warranted and, if so, to be able to make adequate plans about how this is to be conducted.

BOX 5.1	ORGANISED ABUSE

Specific strategies will need to be devised, at this stage, where allegations or suspicions indicate the possibility of organised abuse, involving numbers of children and/or numbers of abusers. This would be true where abuse is suspected in an institutional setting (such as a school or children's home); where it is suspected that a single individual has been abusing a number of children; or where ritual abuse or a paedophile ring may be involved. Such complex cases are inevitably more difficult to investigate and, consequently, the planning and approach of the investigation take on a higher profile. This usually means that managers will get directly involved and the criminal aspects of the case will be given a higher emphasis. For example, the police may set up a criminal investigation team to lead the inquiry.

Where this happens, the tensions between the two functions of the investigation are likely to become especially apparent, and close co-operation and collaboration between social services and the police will be required to ensure that the needs of the children involved do not get compromised in the pursuit of evidence.

Information gathering and processing

The police officer and social worker, both separately and together, now set out to gather the information they need to make well-informed decisions about how to proceed. For example, they may jointly interview the person who made the referral, get detailed information about the child's developmental capabilities (for example, from the child's school, or from the family's health visitor for children under school age) and get specialist advice where necessary (for example, if the child has any disabilities).

At this stage, the child's parent(s) will usually be consulted and, wherever possible, involved in the planning process itself (see Box 5.2). Where a decision is made not to inform or consult the child's parents (and/or others with parental responsibility) because, for example, it is suspected they may have been involved in the abuse, this decision must be justified and a record kept of the reasons. Legal advice would usually be sought if this course of action is to be followed.

BOX 5.2	INFORMING PARENTS AND PARENTAL CONSENT

The Children Act's principle of working together with parents wherever possible is based on the assumption that, in the vast majority of situations, parents have their children's best interests at heart. This inevitably poses problems for those situations where it is a parent or other member of the household who is suspected of harming the child.

In such circumstances, practitioners face the dilemma that what is otherwise 'good practice' – keeping parents fully informed and encouraging their co-operation – may actually increase the danger to the child. For example, it may leave the child vulnerable to coercion or persuasion to retract an allegation, which may involve violence or other threats. The child may be punished for 'disloyalty'. At the least it will alert the family to the investigation, which may lead to evidence being compromised.

It was precisely these kinds of fears which led to the debacles which took place in Cleveland and, more recently, Orkney. Those involved in the investigation were so fearful of such consequences that they acted precipitously by, for example, removing children in 'dawn raids' and denying the children any contact with their families at all.

The Children Act seeks, in a number of ways, to prevent such mistakes happening again. It must be recognised, however, that it does not (and arguably cannot) offer a panacea. The tensions between 'working with the family' and 'protecting the child' are seldom easily resolved in such cases. The best-managed, best-principled practice will always entail making difficult judgements about relative risks. The general public, parents and child-care workers alike have to be prepared to accept that, at times, it may be necessary to act without informing parents or gaining their consent, if children are to be properly protected and not put in further danger.

This is not to condone defensive or autocratic praxis, whereby parents are treated as 'the enemy' and no efforts are made to gain co-operation. Child protection workers have an obligation to conduct investigations in ways that treat children and parents with respect. They must actively seek to avoid underhand, evasive and positively deceitful practices, or simply keeping parents in ignorance to avoid confrontation. Above all, they must be wary of 'jumping to conclusions' and must keep an open mind.

Strategy meeting

Once the information has all been brought together, the substantive strategy meeting can be held, which may well include inputs from other professionals. For example, a paediatrician or child psychiatrist may have valuable inputs to make, especially where there are issues about the child's psychological or emotional state. Three possible decisions may be made on the basis of the information available at this stage:

1   Concerns that were raised about the child are seen to be unfounded and no further action needs to be taken. If the child and parents are aware of the investigation, they will need to be informed about this decision and support may need to be offered to allow them to address the impact of being under suspicion. The person who made the referral should be informed of the outcome.

2   Concerns are not fully allayed, but there appears to be no immediate risk and there is insufficient information to warrant formally continuing the investigation. In this case arrangements will be made to have the child's situation monitored (e.g. by the child's school), but there will be no immediate action to pursue the investigation further. The child and parents should usually be informed that the child's welfare and safety is being monitored, and what form monitoring will take. The person who made the referral should be informed of the outcome. Plans must be made by the local authority to regularly review the child's circumstances and to take appropriate action.

3   The investigation should continue. How this will be approached will depend, critically, on whether or not it proves possible to work in co-operation with the family. A child protection conference may be held at this point, or the police and social services may decide to conduct an investigative interview with the child (see Box 5.3).

If it is decided to go ahead with an interview with the child at this stage, an interview planning meeting will be set up and this may take place immediately. At this meeting the social worker and police officer (again with specialist advice where appropriate) will plan the objectives of the interview and decide on a time, location, who will conduct the interview, who will probably take the lead, and the arrangements that need to be made. Possible further actions (e.g. a medical examination) will be planned for and, again, arrangements set in motion (e.g. contacting the specially trained paediatrician likely to conduct it). Plans for supporting the child will need to be made, including contingency arrangements if a parent is unable to do this.

BOX 5.3 THE CHILDREN'S EVIDENCE PROVISIONS OF THE CRIMINAL JUSTICE ACT 1991

In the 1980s, there were a number of events which highlighted the difficulties that children face when caught up in the criminal justice system, both in terms of the law itself and the practice of interviewers. Grave reservations had been expressed about the manner in which professionals conducted interviews with children. These so-called 'disclosure interviews' came in for much criticism from lawyers. Some judges condemned the interviews as being oppressive and those conducting them as having closed their minds to any explanation of events other than that the children were victims of abuse. They consequently saw the child's evidence as irredeemably tainted by the questioning practices used.

At the same time, the experience of children before the criminal courts had been grounds for concern for much of the 1980s. The Criminal Justice Act 1988 reformed the law by allowing a court to convict on the uncorroborated evidence of a single unsworn child. However, this did not address the issue of the distressing nature of a court appearance for the child who was giving evidence. This was dealt with in part by allowing the child to give evidence by live video-link so that he or she did not have to be in the physical presence of the accused.

It was considered important that the law in its operation should be more child-sensitive; that the practice of those working with children should be geared to enabling children to tell their stories more effectively; that the law should not put up artificial obstacles in the way of such accounts; and that children should be spared the trauma of confrontation in court with their alleged abuser, if at all possible.

In 1988 the Home Office Advisory Group on Video Evidence, chaired by His Honour Judge Pigot, was set up to consider the use of video recordings as a means of taking the evidence of children and other vulnerable witnesses at criminal trials. It reported in December 1989 and contained recommendations which were acted upon (in part) in the Criminal Justice Act 1991.

The Criminal Justice Act 1991 seeks to improve the position of the child giving evidence in criminal proceedings. Centrally, it allows the child witness to give his or her evidence-in-chief by pre-recorded video, *but* the child will still have to be available for cross-examination in order to protect the rights of the accused.

A *Memorandum of Good Practice* has been provided to advise practitioners (notably social workers and police officers) on how to conduct interviews with children, in order to enable the child's account to be used, if necessary, in subsequent criminal proceedings. It recommends that, where there is any possibility of a criminal prosecution, the interview should be video-taped and conducted in a manner which conforms to the rules of evidence for criminal proceedings.

The law over the acceptability of a child's evidence is complex and the *Memorandum of Good Practice* should be consulted for its detail. Here we can only summarise its main features. A child's evidence-in-chief may be accepted in pre-recorded video form only in certain circumstances. These are that the child is:

1   a witness, not the accused;
2   capable of being cross-examined;
3   *either* under fourteen (or if under fourteen when the video was made is now under fifteen), if the offence involves an assault or cruelty to persons under sixteen (section 1 of the Children and Young Person's Act 1933);
    or under seventeen (or if under seventeen when the video was made is now under eighteen), if the offence is a sexual offence.

Parental consent is not required, though desirable. Children must have the purpose of the interview explained to them and, while their formal consent is not required, the interview should not go ahead without their agreement. Appropriate equipment must be used and the tapes securely stored.

The interview should follow a sequence of phases, building from a 'free narrative' account elicited from the child through to open and closed questions and a closure phase. Leading questions will seldom be acceptable and child-facilitative techniques (such as the use of anatomically correct dolls) are specifically discouraged. Wherever possible, only one interview should be conducted and it should not last for longer than about an hour.

Investigative interviewing

If it is decided to conduct an investigative interview, this will now take place, according to the objectives set for it. These will often be somewhat open-ended, in that the risks to the child and the possibility of a criminal prosecution are not likely to be known until the interview is in progress. Consequently, the *Memorandum of Good Practice* will usually be followed and the interview video-taped, wherever possible, to offer the best chance that the child's account can be used as evidence in criminal proceedings.

Planning for the child's protection

Immediately after the interview, the social worker and police officer, together with others where appropriate, will hold a post-interview debriefing. They will review the information gathered and decide what actions need to be taken next. These may include gathering further information (e.g. via a medical examination of the child, interviews with other children or an alleged abuser) and may, in some cases, involve a further interview with the child – in which case another planning meeting will need to be held, usually in consultation with those who can offer specialist advice.

A decision may be made at this point for the police to pursue a criminal investigation and for social services to take immediate legal action to protect the child (e.g. apply for an Emergency Protection Order). Wherever possible, however, they will seek to ensure the child's safety and welfare without removing the child from the family and by working with the family. For example, where a father is suspected of sexually abusing his child, the local authority may offer him accommodation so that he can leave the family home, at least until the investigation is over. The child's mother can be offered social work support and be put in touch with a support group. Alternatively, arrangements may be made for the child to stay with friends or relatives, under close supervision.

Child protection conference

Once all the necessary information is gathered, a child protection conference will usually be held, bringing together all the relevant people and usually involving the parents (see Box 5.4). At this meeting, long-term plans will be made for the child's protection and a decision will be made about whether to place the child's name on the Child Protection Register.

> ### BOX 5.4 ARRANGEMENTS FOR CO-ORDINATING INTER-AGENCY CHILD PROTECTION WORK

Area Child Protection Committees (ACPCs) operate in each area (usually that covered by a local authority). Their main tasks are to establish, maintain and review local inter-agency guidelines on procedures to be followed in individual cases, and to monitor standards of the child protection work carried out in their area. They also review:

- significant issues arising from the handling of particular cases;
- arrangements for access to expert advice and liaison between agencies;
- progress on preventive work;
- inter-agency training.

ACPCs are usually made up of senior officers from each of the agencies involved: social services, the police, hospital and community medical services, education, probation and, where relevant, organisations such as the NSPCC and SSAFA.

A **Child Protection Conference** is usually convened and chaired by the social services department and the main investigative agencies – social services (and the NSPCC where they are involved) and the police will always be involved. Others such as medical and nursing staff, teachers, nursery staff and probation officers will also participate, depending on the circumstances of the case. Increasingly, and in accordance with *Working Together under the Children Act 1989*, parents and children and young people (depending on their age and maturity) will also be invited, and given support to enable them to take part.

The conference is not a court of law and has no legal powers. While the local authority may include their legal representative to advise them about courses of action open to them, in general there is an attempt to avoid any kind of legal 'battle'. Parents are not entitled to be legally represented.

The conference is intended to provide a formal setting within which practitioners and the family can share information and concerns, assess the forms and levels of risk to the child, and make recommendations for action. Conference members pool and discuss a range of information about the child and family under investigation. This usually starts with an account of the precipitating factors that led to the investigation and will include the outcomes of any medical examinations and interviews, if these have been conducted. The child's state of health and development and family's situation will be described, and initial assessment of family functioning and the degree of risk to the child will be made, as far as this is possible.

The only decision that can be made at the conference is whether or not the child's name should be placed on the Child Protection Register and, if so, to allocate a key worker, usually from the social services department, to co-ordinate the case.

The conference also formulates advice to the agencies involved. For example, plans may be made for a detailed assessment of the child and family, and for what will be done to protect the child. The desirability or necessity for legal action to protect the child may also be discussed. While the child protection conference is not empowered to take decisions on such issues (which remain the prerogative of the separate agencies), it is rare for the recommendations of the conference to be overturned.

Increasingly, a core group of professionals most closely involved with the case will be designated by the conference to work together and meet on a regular basis. At periodic intervals (usually every six months), the full conference is reconvened and the situation of the child and family is reviewed. A decision is reached as to the continued need for registration of the child and future plans for inter-agency work agreed by the professionals and the family.

The **Child Protection Register** consists of a centrally kept list of the names and details of children who are believed to be 'at risk' of possible harm. Criteria for registration (normally decided following a child protection conference) as recommended in *Working Together under the Children Act 1989* are:

- physical injury;
- sexual abuse;
- emotional abuse;
- neglect.

Children whose names are registered are those who are living with their families, but where there are unresolved child protection issues. Work will be actively going on to monitor the child's safety and to help parents tackle their problems, according to a plan which sets out what each agency is expected to do, identifies the child's key worker and specifies dates for review.

The Register is maintained in each area on behalf of the Area Child Protection Committee and is usually administered by the social services department. The idea is that the Register provides a central point at which information is kept, which can be checked out whenever a new referral is received. The Child Protection Register also provides a central source of information about the numbers and categories of children registered, and a mechanism for ensuring cases are regularly reviewed.

The Register is kept under strict guidelines of confidentiality and only named professionals in the different agencies have a right of access to the information in it. At the same time, there are arrangements for social services departments to inform each other, for example, if a registered child is moved from one part of the country to another.

Taking appropriate action to protect the child

These actions may range from working with the child and parents to providing alternative care for the child outside the family. Wherever possible, these will be undertaken in partnership with the child's parent(s), but it may be necessary to pursue civil proceedings (e.g. seek a Care Order, see chapter 8).

Usually, a comprehensive assessment will be conducted in order to identify the child's and family's needs for services, following *Protecting Children: A Guide for Social Workers Undertaking a Comprehensive Assessment* (Department of Health, 1987). Services may include treatment and/or therapy for the child and support for the parent(s). These services and the child's welfare and safety will need to be regularly reviewed.

LEGAL REMEDIES FOR CHILD PROTECTION

So far we have concentrated on the ways in which investigations are carried out in co-operation with families, where children are protected while able to continue living with their families. There will always be situations, however, when compulsory intervention is required. The Children Act provides a number of orders which can be used if the investigation is being impeded and/or to remove a child from a situation where they are in danger.

The Child Assessment Order

The Child Assessment Order is intended to tackle circumstances where there are ongoing concerns about a child's long-term health or development, rather than a matter of urgent concern about the child's immediate safety. It is designed primarily to insist that a child is assessed.

C HILD ASSESSMENT ORDER [s43]

Who may apply? The local authority or NSPCC.

Period of Notice: seven days.

Parties: includes the child, and every person whom the applicant believes has parental responsibility for the child. A Guardian ad Litem will be appointed.

Others entitled to notice: includes anybody who has a Contact Order (section 8) or is allowed contact with the child under section 34, a parent without parental responsibility for the child, and every person caring for the child.

Welfare checklist: does not apply, but the presumption of no order [s1(5)] and paramountcy principle [s1(1)] do.

Grounds: The court must be satisfied that the applicant has reasonable cause to suspect that:

1 the child is suffering or is likely to suffer significant harm; *and*
2 an assessment is required to enable the applicant to determine this question; *and*
3 it is unlikely that such an assessment will be made or be satisfactory in the absence of the order.

The court may treat the application as one for an Emergency Protection Order, and should make such an order if its grounds are satisfied and they consider that they ought to do so – in these circumstances the court cannot make a Child Assessment Order.

Powers and duties: The order authorises the applicant to carry out the assessment, and requires any person (in a position to do so) to produce the child for assessment and comply with directions in the order about how the assessment is to be carried out. The child can be kept away from home only if specified in the order and if necessary for the assessment.

The child: may, if 'of sufficient understanding to make an informed decision' refuse to submit to all or part of the assessment.

Duration: Up to a maximum of seven days from a date specified in the order.

Limits: No further application within six months, except by leave of the court.

Challenge: Anyone entitled to notice can apply for variation or discharge of the order. Appeal is to the High Court or Court of Appeal.

The important term in the grounds is 'reasonable cause to suspect', which implies less certainty than 'reasonable cause to believe'. The evidence of harm therefore does not need to be unequivocal. The main thing that the court will need to be convinced about (stressed in *Guidance and Regulations*, Volume 1) is that every reasonable effort has been made to get parental co-operation and this has failed. It is also important to note that as seven-days notice is required, a Child Assessment Order is not practical or appropriate in any situation where there is a chance that a child is at immediate risk.

– HANA'S STORY –

Hana is eighteen months old. Her parents split up six months ago and her father, Frank, is bringing her up on his own. Frank has given up work to be with Hana, who is a demanding and sickly child. Recently she was treated for a severe ear infection.

At first Frank seemed to be coping well, but over the past couple of months the health visitor and social worker have become increasingly concerned about Hana. They are worried about her overall state of health and think she may have a hearing impairment. Certainly, her language development appears very delayed. They have made several appointments to have Hana's hearing checked, but Frank simply fails to turn up. When the health visitor suggested doing the test at home, Frank became antagonistic. He said he couldn't see the point. However hard they tried to persuade him, he refused. He said they were using it as an excuse to take Hana away from him. All efforts to reassure him and all offers of help were refused.

Over most other aspects of Hana's upbringing there seem to be no major problems, but the health visitor and social worker feel that, unless they can do the hearing test, they cannot arrange the kinds of help Hana may need. They discuss the case with their line-managers and decide to apply for a Child Assessment Order.

There are grounds to believe that Hana's health and development could be being impaired by Frank's non-co-operation – several clinic appointments have been missed, Frank has repeatedly refused the health visitor's requests to examine the child when she visits, and he has been repeatedly resistant to offers of support. This combination of circumstances would be sufficient for an order to be sought to allow the necessary assessment to take place.

The Emergency Protection Order

Wherever concerns are more urgent, a Child Assessment Order is not appropriate. For example, it cannot be used to gain access to see a child who is suspected of being at immediate risk. In such a situation, if there were real worries that the child might have been injured or was being severely neglected, an Emergency Protection Order must be sought to gain access to the child.

The Emergency Protection Order is intended to be used for two rather different purposes:

1 by *any person* to deal with an urgent crisis, where a child is in immediate danger, by removing a child from that danger or keeping the child somewhere safe (e.g. a hospital ward);
2 by *a local authority or the NSPCC*, in order to allow them to conduct or continue an investigation when there are immediate concerns about a child's safety.

E MERGENCY PROTECTION ORDER [SS44–45]

Who may apply? Any person for Grounds A; the local authority for Grounds B, the NSPCC for Grounds C.

Period of notice: Applications can be made *ex parte* with leave of the Justices' Clerk. Otherwise, the minimum period of notice is one day.

Parties: includes the child, and every person whom the applicant believes has parental responsibility for the child. A Guardian ad Litem will be appointed.

Others entitled to notice: includes a parent without parental responsibility and any person with whom the child is living or who is providing a refuge.

Welfare checklist: does not apply, but the presumption of no order [s1(5)] and paramountcy principle [s1(1)] do.

Grounds A: Where the applicant is any person, the court must be satisfied that there is reasonable cause to believe that the child is likely to suffer significant harm unless removed to accommodation provided by or on behalf of the applicant, or does not remain in the place where he or she is being accommodated.

Grounds B: Where the applicant is a local authority who is conducting enquiries under section 47(1)(b), the court must be satisfied that:

1 these enquiries are being frustrated by access to the child being unreasonably refused; *and*
2 the local authority has reasonable cause to believe that access to the child is required as a matter of urgency.

Grounds C: Where the applicant is the NSPCC, the court must be satisfied that:

1 the NSPCC has reasonable cause to suspect that the child is suffering or likely to suffer significant harm; *and*
2 the NSPCC is making enquiries with respect to the child's welfare; *and*
3 those enquiries are being frustrated by access to the child being unreasonably refused; *and*
4 the NSPCC has reasonable cause to believe that access to the child is required as a matter of urgency.

Powers and duties: The order authorises the applicant to remove the child from danger or to keep the child in hospital, for example. It provides the applicant with limited parental responsibility.

The court may attach directions allowing or prohibiting a medical examination or other assessment, specifying there is to be no (or curtailed) contact with a named person or persons and that the person enforcing the order be accompanied by a medical practitioner, nurse or health visitor.

The child: may, if 'of sufficient understanding to make an informed decision' refuse to submit to all or part of a medical examination or assessment.

Enforcement: The court may issue a warrant authorising a police constable to assist (using reasonable force if necessary) any person exercising powers under the order, if they are prevented from doing so (e.g. by refusing entry to a home or access to the child).

Duration: up to a maximum of eight days, with the possibility of an extension for a further seven days on application to the court. (Special arrangements are made for public holidays and Sundays). Irrespective of these limits, the child must be returned as soon as it is safe to do so.

Challenge: No application is possible within the first 72 hours of the order, nor by anybody who was given notice of and attended the original hearing, nor to an extension. However, if the child, parent(s) or a person with whom the child was living immediately before the order was made did not attend the original hearing, they may challenge it after 72 hours. There can be an application to vary at any time court directions regarding contact and medical examination, etc of the child.

No appeals are allowed in relation to any aspect of the making or refusal to make an Emergency Protection Order.

The Emergency Protection Order replaces the discredited 'place of safety order' and differs from it in a number of important respects. It lasts for a shorter time, is open to challenge, and assumes children will have contact with their parents unless directions are included to the contrary. The limits of the local authority's powers are clarified, including requiring it to seek authority for a medical examination or other assessment of the child if the results are to be admissible as evidence in Court.

An important innovation is that the grounds are not solely ones of establishing that the child has been/is being significantly harmed, but include the risk that a child *may be* harmed. This is intended to avoid situations where action cannot be taken until the child is actually injured. So long as sufficient evidence can be presented to convince the court that there is reasonable cause to believe that a child *will be significantly harmed*, the order can be made. This might allow, for example, an order to be sought immediately after a child is born, where the mother is a heroin addict.

Police warrants and police protection

It has already been noted that, when an Emergency Protection Order is applied for, a warrant can also be sought for police to accompany the person authorised to remove the child. The warrant allows the accompanying police officer to enter premises and to use reasonable force, if necessary, to gain access to the child – the authorised person does not have these powers [s48].

The police also have the general authority to remove children from danger or prevent their removal to somewhere unsafe if they have 'reasonable cause to believe that a child would otherwise suffer significant harm' [s46(1)]. (Although the Children Act does not authorise the police to enter private property without a warrant, the Police and Criminal Evidence Act 1984 generally permits the police to enter and search premises without a warrant, to 'save life and limb'.)

This is called 'taking the child into police protection' and normally means, in practice, taking the child to a police station (though it can also apply to standing guard over a child in hospital or preventing the removal of a child from a refuge). Once this has been done, the police must:

1. inform the local authority and tell them where the child is being held;
2. inform the child of the steps that have been taken, and what further steps may be taken, if the child appears to be capable of understanding;
3. take reasonably practicable steps to discover the child's wishes and feelings about what has happened;
4. arrange for the child to be moved to local authority accommodation, unless it has already been done or the child is in a refuge (as defined by section 51);
5. inform the child's parents, any others with parental

responsibility, and anybody with whom the child was living immediately beforehand;

6 organise for the case to be taken on by an officer designated by the Chief Constable (usually a police officer designated to specialise in child protection work).

While the child is in police protection, the police do not acquire parental responsibility, but are authorised to 'do what is reasonable in all the circumstances of the case for the purposes of safeguarding or promoting the child's welfare' [s46(9)], taking account of the time the child is likely to remain in police protection. A child cannot be kept in police protection for longer than 72 hours. Usually, well before this time is up, the joint police/social work child-protection team will have taken over responsibility and taken appropriate action. This may involve applying for an Emergency Protection Order.

Local authorities must make arrangements to ensure accommodation is available to take in children who have been placed in police protection. The Act [s47] also places a duty on them to investigate the child's circumstances.

Recovery Order

Where a child is protected by an Emergency Protection Order or in police protection, it is an offence for anybody to take the child away 'without lawful authority or reasonable excuse' [s49(1)]. This also applies to a child who is in the care of the local authority. Where a child is unlawfully removed, or runs away or is missing, a Recovery Order may be sought.

℞ ECOVERY ORDER [s50]

Who may apply? The police (if the child was in police protection) or a local authority (with parental responsibility for the child by virtue of an Emergency Protection or a Care Order).

Period of notice: Applications can be made *ex parte* with leave of the Justices' Clerk. Otherwise the minimum period of notice is one day.

Parties: includes the child, every person whom the applicant believes has parental responsibility for the child, and the person whom the applicant alleges to be responsible for taking or keeping the child. A Guardian ad Litem will be appointed to safeguard the child's interests.

Others entitled to notice: includes any person with whom the child is living and the person providing the refuge.

Welfare checklist: does not apply, but the presumption of no order [s1(5)] and paramountcy principle [s1(1)] do.

Grounds: The court must have reason to believe that the child:

- has been unlawfully taken or kept away from the 'responsible person'; *or*
- has run away or is staying away from the responsible person; *or*
- is missing.

Powers and duties: The order directs any person who is in a position to do so to produce a named child or provide information about the child's whereabouts, authorises the police to enter specified premises to search for the child, and authorises the removal of the child.

Challenge: Appeal is to the High Court or Court of Appeal.

The police, as noted previously, already have a more general authority to enter and search premises and remove children. The main impact of this order, for them, is that it gives them specific authority and requires others to provide them with information.

REFUGES AND SAFE HOUSES

A number of voluntary organisations run 'safe houses', to offer children and young people a place of refuge where they can get away from abusive parents and, importantly, can go to if they are being abused in residential care. The recent Beck and Pin-Down scandals have underlined that this was (and is) a genuine problem that children in care may face. Indeed, the National Association for Young People in Care have always maintained that abuse in care is a far from rare occurrence. Before the Children Act, such 'safe houses' operated on the margins of legality. The Children Act makes specific provisions to enable them to operate legally.

LONG-TERM PROTECTION

The Child Assessment and Emergency Protection Orders offer remedies for short-term protection. Following on from them, the desired outcome is a voluntary set of arrangements, agreed with and developed in partnership with the child's parents, to make sure the child continues to be safe. In other words, wherever possible, the outcome of either order is for the child to be returned to (or stay with) his or her family and for arrangements to be made to protect the child through registration and collaborative work between the various agencies and the family. Where this can be negotiated by working in partnership with the family, this will usually be formalised by the drawing up of a written agreement with the family. Written agreements are not legal contracts and should be thought of more as agreed planning documents. Their purpose is to provide a clearly written statement of what has been negotiated between, for example, the social services and a parent about the way a child will be cared for, what each person will do and what their responsibilities are. Usually an agreement will specify agreed goals, planned outcomes and how they will be achieved.

Obviously, there will always be cases where it is impossible to offer children and young people long-term protection by way of voluntary arrangements, and long-term statutory intervention is required. This is examined in chapter 8.

OTHER REMEDIES

Child protection is predominantly an issue for public law, in terms of the obligations of state agencies to investigate and intervene in cases of child abuse. It is worth briefly mentioning that the law offers some opportunities for private individuals to take action if they are concerned about a child's safety. First, it should be remembered that *any person* can apply for an Emergency Protection Order, but this is rarely likely to be necessary. Generally, the right thing to do will be to make a referral to the police, social services or the NSPCC, to raise concerns with a health visitor (who will usually pass on the referral) or, where people like teachers are concerned, to follow the procedures operating where they work (e.g. set up in the school). Nevertheless, there are occasions where an individual may feel they need to act independently, and the law does allow them to do this. They will need, in the first instance, to contact the Justices' Clerk at their local court, who will advise them what to do.

Another relatively common situation is where a parent is concerned about, for example, what may be happening when the children go to visit their other parent. Here it should be recalled that a Contact Order can be sought to restrict contact or even to prevent it. Children may also, with leave from the court, apply for this order. (Note when children are in care, they may apply for a Section 34 Contact Order to restrict or terminate contact).

PROTECTION FROM INSTITUTIONAL ABUSE

In this chapter we have concentrated mainly on the provisions for protecting children from harm coming from within their families. The Act also makes a number of provisions to protect children from being harmed if they are living in institutions. These are described in chapter 9. It should be noted that an Emergency Protection Order can be sought for a child, irrespective of where they are living – at home, in a boarding school or in a children's home.

6 *Children's welfare and education*

In this chapter we will review those aspects of the law, in relation to children's welfare, which are relevant to those who work in the education sector. This means we will not be concerned with education law (e.g. the various Education Acts) other than how this impinges on welfare. However, because this area involves two different areas of ministerial responsibility with separate legislative programmes which overlap (e.g. the Children Act 1989 and the Education Act 1993), if you have a particular query you should seek further professional advice. Here we will look at the Children Act, both in terms of the impact of its general principles (e.g. the notion of parental responsibility as described in chapter 3) and other more specific elements, such as the new Education Supervision Order.

THE ROLE OF THE EDUCATION SERVICE IN CHILDREN'S WELFARE

While social services are the lead agency for regulating and providing welfare services for children, the Children Act includes a number of provisions which require local education authorities (LEAs) to play a role. Similarly, while the courts are in charge of legal decision-making concerning children's welfare and upbringing, the Children Act also requires LEAs to participate. There are also a number of situations where the powers and duties of LEAs intersect with those of other agencies. We will look at these general provisions for LEA involvement in children's welfare first.

Co-operation and consultation

The Children Act directs social services departments and LEAs to generally assist each other (e.g. by providing information) and to consult with and inform each other whenever one takes action which may affect the other. Whenever social services, for instance, propose to accommodate children in an establishment that provides education, they must, so far as is reasonably practicable, consult the appropriate LEA *before* doing so [s28(1)] and inform the LEA when such arrangements commence and come to an end [s28(2)&(3)]. Equally, whenever an LEA provides children with accommodation for three months or more, or places a child with the intention they will be there for at least that long, they must inform the social services [s85(1)]. The social services department will then be expected to inform itself about the child's welfare and decide if it should take any action [s85(4)].

Children with special educational needs

A clear distinction needs to be drawn between children defined as 'in need' under the Children Act (see chapter 4) and children with 'special educational needs' as defined under the Education Act 1981. While many, if not all, children with special educational needs are likely also to fall within the Children Act definition of 'in need' (if not through disability, then through their need for services), the two definitions serve different purposes and have different implications.

Given the wider scope of the Children Act 'in need' category, many children may be entitled to services as children in need under the Children Act, even though they are not defined as having special educational needs under the Education Act 1981. However, the services to which they are entitled are not the same. Whereas special educational need is specifically linked to *educational* needs, 'in need' is intended to lead to a broader range of support services, to enable families facing troubles of different kinds to look after and care for children themselves.

Having made that distinction, the Department of Education (1989) acknowledges that 'the extent to which a learning difficulty hinders a child's development does not depend solely on the nature and severity of that difficulty'. The help and support provided at home, provision within the school and provision by the LEA and other statutory and voluntary agencies are also relevant. Thus services for children with special educational needs clearly must, under the Children Act, be co-ordinated effectively by collaboration between LEAs and social services departments (and others) in order to meet the children's entitlements (see chapter 4).

The Children Act has, in addition, made some specific provisions for children with special educational needs. Local authorities are given powers to make arrangements to enable a child who has been statemented under section 7 of the Education Act 1981 to attend an establishment outside England and Wales which specialises in providing for children with special needs (for example, the Peto Institute in Hungary). This includes contributing to or paying fees charged by the establishment and reasonable maintenance and travelling expenses [Sched 12, para 36 of the Children Act, inserting a new section 3A into the Education Act 1981]. In addition, it places a general duty on social services departments to 'assist any local education authority with the provision of services for any child within the local authority's area who has special educational needs' [s27(4)].

Representations and complaints

The Children Act requires local authorities and others (e.g. persons running children's homes, which may include small independent boarding schools) to operate and publicise independent procedures for representations and complaints about their services. See chapter 9 for more details of how these must be run.

CHILD PROTECTION

The Department of Education (1991) provides a framework for the involvement of teachers in child protection work and clarifies their responsibilities. Broadly, they are expected to follow the guidance provided in *Working Together under the Children Act 1989* (Department of Health, 1991), which specifies that all schools must appoint a designated teacher who undertakes a liaison role with social services over specific cases and in terms of general consultation. Schools are also expected to have written procedures for how to notify social services (and the NSPCC where relevant) and the police when there are concerns about a pupil's safety and welfare. LEAs are expected to keep and maintain up-to-date registers of designated staff, and to see that they receive appropriate training and support. LEAs, school governors and proprietors of independent schools must make sure their procedures cover cases where a member of staff is alleged to have abused a pupil.

Social services should notify schools (including nursery schools) if a pupil's name has been included on the Child Protection Register, or when a child whose name is on the Register starts school. This notification should include information about whether the pupil is subject to a Care Order, the name of the key worker on the case, and what information may be made known to the parents. Schools are expected to pay particular attention to the attendance and development of such pupils, and to report any cause for further concern to social services. The school must inform the custodian of the Register if the child changes school.

Schools have an important educative role to play in preventing abuse. *Working Together under the Children Act 1989* specifies that schools can do this not only by adopting sound policies and procedures on the management of situations in which there is suspected abuse, but also through the curriculum. They can help pupils to acquire relevant information, skills and attitudes, both to seek help about abuse in their own lives and to prepare them for the responsibilities of their adult lives, including parenthood. The National Curriculum Council has advised that children aged five and above should begin to develop skills and practices that will help them to maintain personal safety as part of school health education and education for citizenship.

Contributing to court proceedings

Under the Children Act, when the welfare or upbringing of a child becomes a matter for court proceedings (whether in public or private law), this is likely to involve education staff in contributing information. For example, the welfare checklist includes a specific reference to children's *educational needs* and, hence, schools, education welfare officers and educational psychologists will usually be expected to provide reports. This is likely to be of particular significance where children have special educational needs or where there are concerns that children between the ages of five and sixteen are not being properly educated.

Moreover, given that courts will set timetables for proceedings, specify what information needs to be gathered and schedule its provision, education staff will be expected to provide these reports within tightly specified timescales and to closely defined briefs.

– COLLIN'S STORY –

Collin is fourteen, and is currently living with his older sister, Eve, following an argument with his parents after the police brought him home late one night when he was very drunk. Both his mother and father say they want him back, but fear they simply cannot cope with Collin any longer. They contacted social services, saying they are very worried about what is going on at his sister's. They have very little contact with her. They say she is a drug addict and setting Collin a bad example.

The local authority begin to investigate and are unhappy about the situation. Eve does not appear to be coping at all well with Collin. He seems to be running out of control and she says he is not her responsibility. His teachers at school say Collin is truanting most of the time and becoming increasingly disruptive when he does come to school. He has been caught on several occasions glue sniffing, and they think he may be taking other illegal drugs. They are considering excluding him from the school.

The local authority decides to apply for a Care Order. At the directions appointment, a date is set six weeks hence for a final hearing. Collin's school have been asked to report on Collin's educational needs and their plans for him, and the LEA have been asked to make a report outlining whether it would be possible for Collin to be placed in a school for young people with behavioural problems. These reports must be submitted to the court within three weeks.

In cases like this, schools and LEAs will need to be able to respond quickly and efficiently. They must have in place a system for preparing reports (and getting legal advice if needed) according to strict timetables, prepared by people who can demonstrate the expertise and qualifications required to do so with authority – remember, these judgements can be challenged in court. In Collin's case, the LEA and the school will have some difficult decisions to make. With the pressure of the court timetable, they will need to act fast. Note also that care proceedings are 'specified proceedings' and therefore a Guardian ad Litem will be appointed to safeguard Collin's best interests.

IMPACT OF THE CHANGES OVER PARENTHOOD

As was noted in chapter 3, 'parental responsibility' has become something which endures throughout a child's minority and is not lost following parental divorce or when a child is made the subject of a Care Order, even though it may be shared (for example, with the local authority). LEAs and schools therefore need to keep up-to-date records of all the people who have parental responsibility for each of their pupils. For example, where a pupil's parents are divorced, the school should keep details of the names and addresses of both parents.

Parental responsibility for children 'in care'

The situation is more complicated for children being looked after by the local authority (see chapters 4 and 8) in that the local authority will have parental responsibility only for those who are 'in care'. Although they share this with the child's parent(s), in practice this will generally mean that over most day-to-day issues (e.g. giving consent for a pupil to go on a school trip) it will be the local authority who will have the authority to give permission. However, in terms of making more far-reaching decisions about the child (e.g. a decision to change school), both the local authority and the child's parents will need to be consulted. Schools therefore need to keep accurate, up-to-date records of the children who are in the care of the local authority.

Parental responsibility for other children

Those children who are accommodated (and those previously in 'voluntary care') are not 'in care' and, hence, the local authority will not have parental responsibility for them. A number of other people (e.g. relatives or foster-parents) may acquire parental responsibility for children by being awarded a Residence Order. Unmarried fathers can also gain parental responsibility by a court order or formal agreement with the child's mother.

Implications for the education sector

All those with parental responsibility must be treated equally by schools and LEA staff, unless there exist court orders limiting individuals' exercise of their parental responsibility. All are entitled, for instance, to vote in elections for parent governors or ballots concerning the school's status, and to participate in assessments for special educational needs. All are entitled to receive school reports if they request them. If any person contacts a school claiming to have parental responsibility, the school will need to establish whether or not this is so (e.g. by consulting the County or Borough Solicitor's Office).

Impact of section 8 orders following parental separation

In chapter 3 we examined the ways in which section 8 orders may be used to determine disputes over a child's upbringing. The awarding of a section 8 order will often have implications for a child's education. Schools (and other education staff where relevant) therefore need to include in pupils' records details of any section 8 order made and any conditions or directions that have been made by the court.

– LEAH'S STORY –

Leah is seven. Her parents divorced last year and were unable to agree over where she would live. Her mother, Mirriam, applied for a Residence Order and one was made in her favour. Leah's father, David, was awarded a Contact Order, which specified Leah would go to stay with him every other weekend and for a minimum of three weeks over the summer holiday.

Mirriam tells Leah's teacher she is worried that David may be planning to take Leah away on holiday in school time, which she does not agree with. Sure enough, David writes to the headteacher, saying he is planning a trip to the Lake District in June, and asking permission for Leah to miss two weeks of the summer term.

In this situation Mirriam is entitled to refuse permission for Leah to miss school, as David's Contact Order only allows him to take Leah for a holiday out of term time. The school would be prudent to consult with Mirriam and, if she says she does not consent to the plan, to inform David of this. It is then up to the parents to resolve the matter. David could apply to the court for a Specific Issue Order to allow him to take Leah at the time he plans. In this case, the school may well be asked to advise the court about the potential benefits of the holiday and the potential harms of missing school for Leah.

Whatever section 8 orders are in force, *both* parents should be consulted about all major decisions about their children (e.g. a decision about changing school or removing a child from religious education). If parents get into dispute about such decisions, they can apply to the court for resolution. A Specific Issue Order would allow one parent to agree, for example, to a pupil changing school against the wishes of the other parent. A Prohibited Steps Order would allow one parent to prevent a child from attending a form of religious worship that the other parent wished the child to attend.

Authority to act without parental responsibility

Education staff do not have 'parental responsibility', as defined by the Children Act, for the pupils in their care. Those with parental responsibility may not surrender or transfer any part of it to another, but may arrange for some or all of it to be met by one or more persons acting on their behalf [s2(9)]. Thus parents may give authority to schools to act *in loco parentis*.

The Children Act does, however, allow a school to take independent action towards a pupil to deal with emergencies. The Act states that a person 'who does not have parental responsibility for a particular child; but ... has care of the child, may (subject to the provisions of this Act) do what is reasonable ... for the purpose of safeguarding or promoting the child's welfare' [s3(5)]. In this context, 'has care of' applies to activities such as child-minding and pastoral care within school, on school trips, and so on.

– NGUYEN'S STORY –

Nguyen is nine. He goes away with the school on a day trip to the Zoo. While playing in the Zoo's adventure playground he falls over and cuts his knee rather badly. His teacher takes him to the first aid post and they recommend he goes to hospital.

The teacher in charge tries to call Nguyen's parents, but they have also gone away for the day and cannot be contacted. The teacher is satisfied she has the authority to take the child to hospital, as it seems an eminently 'reasonable' thing to do for the child's welfare.

It needs to be noted, though, that this clarification of a teacher's right to take action in emergency situations is limited by the caveat 'subject to the provisions of this Act'. This means that it will be unlawful to act in ways that directly infringe any of the Act's requirements, and parents will still need to be consulted about most decisions made on a pupil's behalf. It will only be lawful to act without parental consent being obtained if, as is the case with Nguyen, a pupil needs urgent medical attention and the parent(s) cannot be contacted. This authority to act without parental consent is also important with regard to child protection, and we will come back to it later in this chapter.

The Children Act's incorporation of the notion of the 'mature minor' is also relevant. The mature minor is regarded as competent to agree to medical treatment without needing the consent of whoever has parental responsibility for him or her. This does not mean that it is wise to dispense with the need for parental consent in usual circumstances. Nonetheless, this feature of the Act does offer education staff some flexibility in ambiguous situations and does mean that mature pupils will have some freedom to make certain decisions for themselves, independently from their parents.

– BRIDGET'S STORY –

Bridget is fifteen and in the fifth form at school. She is not 'in care', but has been accommodated by the local authority for five years now. She lives in a children's home. Up until recently she lived with foster-parents, but she was unhappy there and asked to be moved. The local authority were obliged to take her wishes and feelings into account and so agreed to her choice not to live with a family. Bridget has a boyfriend, and recently went to her GP and asked to be put on 'the pill'. After talking with her, the GP agreed and said that she accepted Bridget did not want her parents to know.

Bridget is about to be entered for her GCSE exams. She is angry that she is forced to take subjects she does not like. She says it's her future at stake and, if she's old enough to decide where she lives and to be given contraception, why isn't she considered old enough to decide what exams she takes?

Here we can see the tensions between the two quite different ways that welfare and education law construct children – welfare law acknowledges children's growing autonomy, whereas education law stresses 'parental choice'. It is little wonder that children, themselves, are confused.

LEGAL REMEDIES OVER EDUCATIONAL MATTERS

In this section we will examine ways that schools and LEAs can seek remedies if they are concerned about some aspect of a child's education. What follows is not exhaustive – for example, concerns regarding truancy can give rise not only to an application for an Education Supervision Order, but also to a Care Order or the criminal prosecution of the parents.

Using section 8 orders

As was noted in chapter 3, section 8 orders can be used by a public body (for example, a local authority or health authority), where it is felt that parental authority needs to be challenged in order to promote or safeguard a child's welfare. LEAs may seek Prohibited Steps or Specific Issue Orders in order to address aspects of a pupil's education over which they have concerns, or decisions that parents have made.

A Specific Issue Order might be appropriate, for example, where an assessment of a child's special educational needs made under the Education Act 1981 establishes that a particular kind of school will best meet a child's needs, but the parents refuse permission for the child to move to the school or even to discuss the matter. If made by a court, a Specific Issue Order could overturn the parents' objection and direct that the child attend the school. All other aspects of parental responsibility would be unaffected. The welfare checklist would apply if the parents contested the order. The LEA would therefore need to prepare a detailed account of the child's educational needs, its assessment of where the child should be educated, and what assistance it has offered to make this possible. It would need to explain why the parents were unable and/or unwilling to meet these needs without the order being made, and what harm the child was thereby suffering or had suffered. An alternative might be to apply for an Education Supervision Order.

The Education Supervision Order

Although LEAs retain their power to prosecute parents under the Education Act 1944 [ss37 or 39] if children in their area are failing to attend school, they now, under the Children Act, have two other courses of action which are likely to be more appropriate. First, the LEA can report its concerns to social services for them to investigate. This will be the most suitable course of action when it is considered that the child's non-attendance at school arises from other problems in the family (for example, where parents are neglecting their children or expecting them to stay home from school to care for younger siblings). Social services would then be under a duty to investigate the child's circumstances (see chapter 7). Second, they may apply for an Education Supervision Order.

*E*DUCATION SUPERVISION ORDER [s36]

Who may apply? The LEA where the child is living, will live, or where the child is a registered pupil at a school. The LEA *must* consult the appropriate social services committee.

Period of notice: seven days

Parties: The child, and every person whom the applicant believes has parental responsibility for the child.

Others entitled to notice: includes the person with whom the child is living.

Welfare principle: The welfare checklist does apply, as do the presumption of no order [s1(5)] and paramountcy principle [s1(1)].

Grounds: The court must be satisfied that:

- the child is of compulsory school age; *and*
- the child is not receiving efficient, full-time education suitable to his or her age, ability and aptitude and any special educational needs he or she may have.

This order cannot be made in respect of a child who is in local authority care.

Powers and duties: The order places the child under the supervision of the LEA. The child's supervisor is under a duty to advise, assist, befriend and give direction to the child and parent(s) in such a way as to secure that the child is properly educated.

While the supervisor must give due consideration to the wishes of the child and parents about where the child is to be educated, the parents lose their right under the 1980 Education Act to choose their child's school.

The supervisor may direct that the child is medically examined or assessed (e.g. by an educational psychologist).

The child: may, if 'of sufficient understanding to make an informed decision', refuse to submit to the examination or assessment.

Duration: Up to one year initially, but extensions up to three years may be made on application of the LEA. It ends when the child ceases to be of compulsory school age, or on the making of a Care Order.

Challenge: The child, parent(s) or LEA can apply for discharge of the order. Appeal is to the High Court.

Before applying for an Education Supervision Order, all reasonable efforts must have been made to resolve the problems that are causing the child to fail to receive proper education.

– CRESSIDA'S STORY –

Cressida is eleven and lives with her parents and grandparents in an isolated farmhouse. Cressida started to attend the nearest primary school, six miles from home, at the age of five, but a year ago her parents removed her from the school and said they would educate her at home.

The educational welfare officer has made several visits to the family. She reports that Cressida appears to be doing well in educational terms and is performing well for her age. However, she is worried that Cressida is becoming very isolated, as she hardly ever meets other children of her age.

Cressida should have moved up to secondary school this term and the LEA feels that her educational needs cannot be properly met by her parents now Cressida has reached secondary school age. All attempts to negotiate with her parents have failed. Cressida herself seems to be being put under pressure, and has privately said to the educational welfare officer that she would like to go to school so she can make friends.

In a case like this, the decision made by the court will depend on the grounds for an Education Supervision Order being satisfied, and on consideration of the welfare checklist. If the grounds are satisfied, the Education Supervision Order can be made. If the grounds are not satisfied, but the court is sufficiently concerned about her other needs and is mindful of her own wishes and feelings, they may make a Specific Issue Order, directing that Cressida's parents should send her to school. However, the court will need to be convinced that making an order is better for her than making no order at all.

Supervising an Education Supervision Order
The supervisor appointed may be an educational welfare officer or an education social worker. However, if appropriate, and if the

necessary arrangements can be made, the task may be delegated to a social worker who knows the family and has established a working relationship with them.

An Education Supervision Order gives a supervisor very considerable discretion about directions to be made, which can be to the pupil or parent(s) or both. Directions may include requirements to attend meetings at regular, specified intervals to discuss the child's progress with the supervisor or with specified teachers; or for the pupil to be medically examined or assessed by an educational psychologist. A supervisor may arrange education other than at a school and direct that the pupil participate (i.e. using the LEA's powers under section 56 of the Education Act 1944).

Where there is more than one Supervision Order in force

There may be cases where an Education Supervision Order and a Supervision Order (see chapter 8) or a Criminal Supervision Order (obtained under section 7 of the Children and Young Persons Act 1969) are operating in parallel for a particular child. Arrangements will need to be made for supervision to be shared or at least co-ordinated, with clear understanding of common goals and specific roles.

BOARDING SCHOOLS

The Children Act has made significant changes to the regulations governing boarding schools. These are dealt with in chapter 9, when we look at children living away from home.

7 *Children's welfare and health*

This chapter is about the ways that child welfare law is relevant to those who work in the health sector.

PROVISION OF WELFARE SERVICES

In the UK, health care is (in theory at least) a universal welfare service provided to all children. Indeed, people take it so much for granted that it is often not seen as 'welfare'. Consequently, it does not carry the same kind of stigma as services (like social work support) which are targeted on just some families. While, in practice, this may be changing somewhat (given the erosion of resources and the changes in systems of provision), this lack of stigma is an important factor in the role that health professionals can play in offering welfare support to families and in child protection. Parents generally do not feel as threatened, for example, by a visit from a health visitor as they may do by a visit from a social worker. Similarly, families where a child is disabled do not usually see themselves as receiving charity, but as receiving services to which they and the child are entitled.

Thus, while social services are the lead agency for regulating and providing general welfare services for children 'in need' (see chapter 4) and the key agency in the co-ordination of preventive work with 'at risk' children on child protection registers (see chapter 5), in many cases it will be health professionals who take on the main direct work with the children and families concerned. Again, the effective provision of welfare services to children is reliant on close working partnerships – here between social services and health agencies.

Identification and assessment of children in need

Given that right from birth all children have contact with health services, more often than not this will be where the possibility will first be raised that a child may need services in order to promote his or her health and development. Certainly this will be the case with the vast majority of children with disabilities, and will very often be the case for younger children with more 'social' needs. Where a child's disability is detected at birth, it will generally be hospital staff who will need to inform the local authority. Needs identified later in a child's life are more likely to be picked up by the family's GP or health visitor.

Both sectors of health care play a critical role in helping to make sure that all children get the services to which they are entitled in law. This means thinking beyond those health-care services which they provide directly. The Children Act places specific duties on local authorities to see that every child living in their area has the basic living conditions that they need for healthy development. Of course, actually getting these entitlements will often prove difficult in practice, given the resource limitations under which local authorities operate. However, this should not stop health professionals from taking the initiative, by telling parents about their rights, by alerting social services, and by giving the information required to make cases for services to be provided.

– JANE'S STORY –

Jane is a premature baby and is spending her first few weeks of life in a special care unit in hospital. The paediatrician in charge of her case has become very concerned about the living conditions to which the baby will be discharged in a few days' time. Jane's parents are living in bed-and-breakfast accommodation. They occupy a single bedroom with their two older children, Phillip (aged two) and Mary (aged four). This room is damp and small, with nowhere for the younger children to play. The family share a bathroom and kitchen on another floor with two other families.

In the paediatrician's view, the cramped and unhygienic conditions in which the family are living are totally unsuitable to meet Jane's needs. If she is to have any hope of healthy development, the family need to be rehoused. The paediatrician discusses her concerns with Jane's parents and, with their agreement, contacts social services. She writes a report setting out a clear case that Jane is a child 'in need' and that, without adequate housing, her health and development are likely to be significantly impaired.

Of course, whether the family will be rehoused is another matter. Nevertheless, health professionals have a key role to play in alerting social services about children's health needs and providing information which will enable social workers to make a case for resource allocation.

Providing services for children in need

As we saw in chapter 4, the Act places duties on local authorities to provide appropriate services for children in need.

– JEREMY'S STORY –

Jeremy was born with Down's syndrome. He had a mild degree of learning disability, but was otherwise healthy. He is the fourth child in the family. His brother and two sisters were teenagers when he was born, his mother was in her forties and his father in his late fifties.

When Jeremy grew up and went to school, he developed a strong enjoyment of music. He learned to play the piano and his parents paid for him to have lessons. He also played recorder in the school band. At this point in his life he was a happy and contented lad, who enjoyed being 'spoiled' by the rest of his family.

Sadly, when Jeremy was eleven he suffered from meningitis and was left with a severe hearing loss. He is now twelve. He cannot play his instruments, he has been placed in a special school away from all his friends, and it is as though all the joy has gone out of his life. His brother and sisters have, by now, left home and he is very lonely. His father, now well into his sixties, is himself disabled. His mother is finding it very difficult to manage with both of them, as Jeremy often gets extremely frustrated and is becoming violent towards her. The parents consult their GP and ask her whether it would be possible to arrange for Jeremy to go into a home, as they feel they will not be able to cope with him much longer.

Jeremy's needs will have been assessed soon after birth and regularly thereafter. Social services, health and education agencies, alongside voluntary organisations, should have worked together to provide the services that he and his family needed. The local authority is under a statutory duty to provide services designed to minimise the effects on him of his disabilities, to give him the opportunity to lead a life which is 'as normal as possible' [Sched 2, para 6], and to promote his upbringing by his family [s17(1)].

Clearly, in a case like this, health services will be critical both for Jeremy and his parents. Assessment will need to include both strictly medical needs and social needs. What this family will require are a clear set of options, which may range from support within the family, through respite care, to a place for Jeremy in a suitable residential establishment where, for example, he can be helped to continue with his musical interests. While the Act states a preference for Jeremy to stay in his family, this may need to be looked at in terms of Jeremy's future, given that his parents will be justifiably concerned about the time when they can no longer look after him.

In a case like this, Jeremy's future wellbeing and happiness will depend upon the ability of different agencies to work together with each other and in genuine partnership with his parents. If the right mix of services can be identified and provided, there is every reason to hope that Jeremy and his family can look forward to a worthwhile and satisfying future for him. If this cannot be achieved, his future may be very bleak and his parents may suffer considerable distress.

Assessment
Assessment is a key element in service provision. It is important both in terms of establishing the needs of individual children and

in enabling local authorities to plan and deliver an appropriate level and range of services in their locality. Clearly, health professionals have a central role to play in assessment. They have particular forms of knowledge and skill which will often be critical in identifying the needs of particular children and their families, and in establishing how these needs can be met. At the same time, assessment will always need to be a shared process, given that other agencies will also have their own knowledge and skills to contribute.

In particular, the Act specifies that assessment under its provisions may be carried out in conjunction with other assessments conducted under the Chronically Sick and Disabled Persons Act 1970; the Education Act 1981, the Disabled Persons (Services, Consultation and Representation) Act 1986, and any other enactment [Sched 2, para 3]. Thus, in the case of disabled children and/or disabled parents, it will make sense to co-ordinate the assessment process – to avoid duplication, but also to make sure that it is properly done.

Health professionals therefore need to establish procedures and working partnerships which will enable them to contribute to individual assessments of particular children and their families, case by case, and to systematic planning and service provision within the locality.

Registration

The Act requires local authorities to identify all the children in need in their area [Sched 2, para 1(1)], to set up and maintain a register of disabled children [Sched 2, para 2) and to publicise the services available [Sched 2, para 1(2)]. While social services will be the lead agency in charge of these responsibilities, health services will clearly need to be very much involved. Once again, effective co-operation and collaboration will make all the difference in enabling these tasks to be carried out effectively. It is important to note that a child does not have to be on the register in order to receive services.

CONSENT TO MEDICAL EXAMINATIONS AND TREATMENT

Usually, when children are medically examined or given medical treatment, it is by the consent of their parents. The Children Act's changes concerning parenthood therefore clearly affect the way that medical professionals deal with child patients. What will be critical is knowing, for each child, who has parental responsibility, because, in the usual course of events, it will only be those with parental responsibility who have authority to give consent to examination and treatment.

– KORVINDA'S STORY –

Korvinda is ten years old. Her parents are divorced and she has gone to live with her mother at her grandparents' house. Korvinda's mother has a Residence Order in her favour, specifying that this is where Korvinda will live.

One morning Korvinda is brought to the health centre by her grandmother, who wants to arrange for the child to have the necessary inoculations for a trip that she will be making with her mother to Pakistan.

Consent in non-urgent cases

Korvinda's grandmother does not have parental responsibility and so cannot consent to the doctor giving Korvinda the inoculations. This will need to be explained to the grandmother and arrangements made for the mother to give her consent. Alternatively, Korvinda's mother can arrange for the grandmother to act on her behalf [s2(9)], by giving her authority to consent to the child receiving medical treatment. If so, the staff at the centre would be wise to have this confirmed in writing. If, however, Korvinda's grandmother had been given a Residence Order in her favour, this would have given her parental responsibility so that she could then, in her own right, authorise medical examination or treatment.

If a person with parental responsibility objects

If Korvinda's father were to object – for example, if he were concerned about the proposed trip – he might call the health centre and ask them not to proceed. In law, Korvinda's mother can act independently – the father's permission is not necessary. However, if this happened, it would be prudent for staff at the centre to wait for a while. Hopefully the parents would be able to sort out their dispute between themselves, but Korvinda's father could seek a Prohibited Steps Order (see chapter 3) to prevent the inoculations being given.

Authority to act in cases of emergency

The situation is different in the case of a child needing urgent medical treatment. For example, if Korvinda's grandmother took her to hospital with a serious injury which needed emergency treatment, the grandmother's consent would fall within the Act, which states that a person who is caring for a child but does not have parental responsibility for that child may, subject to the provisions of the Act, 'do what is reasonable in all the circumstances of the case for the purposes of safeguarding or promoting the child's welfare' [s3(5)]. This enables anybody who can be regarded as having the care of a child – not only a relative, but a teacher, child-minder or, indeed, a doctor receiving a child into casualty – to, in extreme circumstances, take action which is clearly necessary to save a child's life or treat serious injury. If the need to act is very urgent, it is not essential to try to get consent from somebody with parental responsibility. Of course, where there is less urgency, it will always be better to try to do so if at all possible, certainly with younger children. (We look at the child's ability to give consent a little later in this chapter).

Limits on authority to act without parental consent

The caveat 'subject to the provisions of the Act' is important. It means that a caregiver cannot, in usual circumstances, act in ways which would undermine or go against the wishes of the person(s) with parental responsibility for the child. Thus, even if the grandmother had been given delegated authority by the child's mother, she could not try to arrange for Korvinda to have inoculations if she knew neither of Korvinda's parents wanted this to happen. Similarly, if a child's parents were known to have religious objections to certain forms of treatment – such as a blood transfusion – then it would be unlawful to go against those known wishes. Rather, where a child's life will be endangered unless such treatment is given, the medical staff concerned would need to apply to the court for a Specific Issue Order, to gain the authority to go ahead.

A child's ability to give or refuse consent

A milestone in legal history was reached with the Gillick appeal ruling in 1986 in the House of Lords. Up until that point it had generally been assumed that, while young people over the age of sixteen were able to give consent, in their own right, to medical examinations or treatment, a child below the age of sixteen could not. At issue in the Gillick case was whether or not a medical practitioner was able to offer confidential advice about contraception to young people who were under sixteen, who refused for their parents to be consulted or even told. The ruling established that such action can be lawful.

Consent to medical treatment
Its effect is that children and young people, once they are deemed to be of sufficient understanding to be capable of making up their own mind on a matter and fully understand what is involved, are generally seen as lawfully competent to make decisions for themselves. In general, this is taken to mean that they can give consent to medical treatment. Specifically, under the Children Act, unless a child who is of sufficient understanding to make an informed decision consents to being medically or psychiatrically treated, such a requirement cannot be made under a Supervision Order [Sched 3, para 5(5)(a)].

Refusal of medical treatment
It might be thought that, given their ability to give consent, young people who are regarded as 'Gillick competent' would also be seen as equally able to refuse medical treatment. However, a number of recent cases have shown that this is not

the case. In a recent case the Court of Appeal decided that a sixteen-year-old's right to consent to medical treatment did not mean she had a power of veto over such treatment. A person with parental responsibility or the court has the power to give effective consent, thus overriding even a mature minor's refusal.

Refusal to submit to a medical examination

The situation becomes all the more complicated when we consider a child's ability to refuse to submit to a medical examination. Here, the Children Act is quite clear. In circumstances where directions may be given that a child is medically or psychiatrically examined or otherwise assessed – in the making of a Child Assessment Order [s43(8)], an Emergency Protection Order [s44(7)], or an interim Care or Supervision Order [s38(6)] – the Act gives children and young people who are of 'sufficient understanding to make an informed decision' the right to refuse to submit to an examination or other assessment. Similarly, directions for medical examination within a Supervision Order cannot be made unless the child with the requisite understanding consents [Sched 3, para 4(4)(a)].

However, in another recent case the High Court made it clear that, despite the wording of the Act, the High Court still has the power under its inherent jurisdiction to override the child's refusal if it thinks this is in the child's best interests. We will return to this issue in chapter 10.

Consent to medical examination

The Gillick ruling and Children Act provisions have so far been generally taken to mean that children and young people who are capable of making an informed decision can consent, in their own right, to being medically examined. This suggests, in principle, that medical examinations can be carried out with 'mature minors' without consulting with parents or seeking their consent, so long as the child consents. However, especially in cases of suspected sexual abuse which might result in criminal proceedings against a parent, this course of action is open to challenge and should only be followed with extreme caution, particularly where younger children are concerned. We will return to this matter later in this chapter.

BOX 7.1   BEFORE UNDERTAKING A MEDICAL EXAMINATION

Before undertaking any medical examination or other assessment with a child, all medical practitioners should ask:

- Who has the right to consent to this examination or assessment?
- Who has parental responsibility for this child?
- What are the child's views about the examination?
- Does the child have any difficulties in communication? If so, do special arrangements need to be made?
- Is the child subject to a court order? If so, has the court made directions in the order? If so, what are they?
- Has a Guardian ad Litem been appointed? If so, what are his or her views?
- Will the assessment be used in court proceedings? Are there circumstances in which it could be used?

This list is based on the Department of Health's *The Children Act 1989: An Introductory Guide for the NHS* (pp. 32–3)

Concerns about a child's health

Cases of alleged child assault or where a child needs life-saving treatment for which parents refuse consent are, happily, relatively rare occurrences. More common are circumstances where health professionals are generally concerned about a failure or unwillingness on the part of parents to co-operate with medical treatment or health care of a less urgent nature, or simply when they fail to bring the child for medical checks and examinations. In such cases the issue will turn on whether the child's health or development is being, or is likely to be, significantly harmed by this lack of parental co-operation – in other words, whether a case can be made for child protection measures.

At first sight, it may appear to be an over-reaction to suggest that a lack of compliance with medical treatment or health care may be a case of 'child abuse'. However, two points are worth bearing in mind. First it must be remembered that, where a child's health is at stake, the first duty of any professional must always be to the child patient. Second, such non-compliance can, on occasions, arise because there are other problems in the family. Medical staff will, in many situations, be the first to notice that something untoward is going on. Sensitive but decisive action can often catch a problem before it becomes too serious. At times it can be critical in preventing a tragedy.

– BEN'S STORY –

Ben is nine years old and he lives with his mother and father. Two years ago he was diagnosed as diabetic. He now receives daily insulin and is supposed to be kept on an appropriate diet.

At first his parents were very anxious and concerned, and almost too co-operative, though Ben appeared to be coping well. In the last few months, however, his condition seems to be taking a downturn. On his last two clinic visits, weight loss has been noticed. Checks on his blood-sugar levels show rather poor levels of control and marked deterioration has been noticed in his appearance. His mother said she is making sure he gets his insulin, but she is 'fighting a losing battle' over his eating. After questioning, she rather grudgingly admitted that he has become 'very disobedient and naughty' and is in trouble at school.

When the doctor tried to talk about Ben's behaviour, his mother became very defensive. She said she accepted she needed to get medical help for Ben's condition, but it was not the doctor's job to tell her how to bring up her own son. When the doctor asked to talk to Ben on his own, his mother refused and said, angrily, that her son had nothing to say that he could not say in front of her.

Ben and his mother failed to attend the next two check-ups and the staff are now getting very concerned. Attempts to arrange a home visit by the liaison nurse have been met with antagonism and she has so far failed to get to see Ben. His mother said on the telephone that it was not convenient to see the liaison nurse at any of the times suggested. She promised to bring Ben to the clinic today, but so far they have not shown up.

The options in a case like this will depend upon the doctor's clinical judgement of the urgency of the situation and the potential for harm. If concerns are very serious and urgent, then an Emergency Protection Order could be sought. For example, if there are real worries that a diabetic child may be failing to get his or her insulin, this may be the only safe course of action. In less urgent cases a Child Assessment Order may be more appropriate. However, this takes time, as notice must be served on the parents, and would not be appropriate where there was any need for prompt intervention. (These orders are discussed in detail in chapter 5.)

These, of course, are serious measures and difficult for medical staff to pursue independently (though any person may apply for an Emergency Protection Order if they believe a child is in real and immediate danger). The doctor could seek to work through the local GP or health visitor, especially if they have an established working relationship with the family. However, he or she may be better advised to contact social services. They would then be under an obligation to investigate the child's circumstances [s47] and would, for example, be in a better position to check things out with the child's school and see whether there were any other matters of concern in the family. Moreover, social services will have specialist staff with expertise in child protection work and access to legal advice. In a case like this, it would be critical for the two agencies to work closely together, and for social services to be made aware of the nature and urgency of the clinical concerns.

Medical examinations in cases of suspected child abuse

We examine child protection issues for health professionals later in this chapter. While we are on the subject of medical examinations, however, it is worth making some points about situations where these are conducted as part of an investigation of possible child abuse.

In cases of physical trauma, medical staff are in a relatively clear-cut situation. Their first duty will be to their child patient, and they will be acting well within their authority to examine any child brought to them suspected of suffering from such things as fractures, poisoning, severe bruising or other serious injuries. Here the issue will seldom be one of parental consent, but what action they must take if they suspect the injury is non-accidental. Where a parent does seek to frustrate an examination that in a physician's clinical judgement is necessary, then this is, in itself, a very worrying sign. Immediate steps will need to be taken to protect the child. If, for example, the parent tries to remove the child, the police can be called (see chapter 5).

In cases where the concern is more one about long-term neglect, the situation is likely to be different because this will seldom be a matter of urgency. Rather, the task is to monitor for medical signs of deterioration or failure to thrive. If these become serious, or the parent(s) persistently fail to attend for checks, social services will need to be informed and the case will become one for inter-agency child protection.

The situation is, however, more complex where there are allegations or suspicions of sexual abuse. The reason is that, in this sort of case, medical examination may fulfil two quite different purposes. First, it has the usual function of establishing whether the child is in need of medical treatment. Second, it may also be critical in the provision of evidence, which may be used in child protection proceedings *and* in criminal proceedings. Because of the latter, parents may sometimes seek to prevent a medical examination from being conducted or to delay it happening. Given that forensic evidence of sexual assault may depend, critically, on conducting an examination soon after the alleged assault occurred, this may pose a serious problem.

In such situations, it may be far more difficult to justify a medical examination solely in terms of the child's health needs. Yet, the provision of evidence may be critical in protecting the child in the future. The best advice in cases like these is to seek expert advice from a lawyer as a matter of urgency. In any case forensic medical examination is a skilled and specialist task and should not be undertaken by anyone without adequate training. This holds true for any examination which may involve the production of evidence. It is particularly true where there is an issue over consent.

THE ROLE OF HEALTH PROFESSIONALS IN CHILD PROTECTION

As has already been explained in chapter 5, social services have a statutory obligation to investigate the circumstances of any child who is the subject of an Emergency Protection Order, is in police protection, or who they otherwise suspect may be suffering from (or at risk of suffering) significant harm [s47(1)]. Furthermore, it is social services who will usually be in charge of maintaining and operating Child Protection Registers and administering the Area Child Protection Committee, and generally taking action for the protection of children. In some areas they may delegate some of these responsibilities to the NSPCC. Nonetheless, health professionals have crucial roles to play in child protection.

Prevention

A great deal of the work that is done with children and families by health professionals can be seen as preventive. Helping families to gain access to resources and services will often play a highly significant role in stemming problems before they become serious. It is worth noting, for example, that in studies of mothers who mistreat their children it is often found that the mother is suffering from quite minor (but nonetheless debilitating) health problems, such as toothache. Similarly, studies of under-fives who have suffered from non-accidental injury suggest that many of them have problems with sleeping or persistent crying, caused, for example, by colic. Thus, while not falling in any obvious way under the legal definition of 'services for children and families', effective routine health care can be a critical factor in promoting and safeguarding a child's welfare.

Identification of children who may be at risk

Health professionals are closely involved with children at birth and in the immediate period afterwards. Health visitors, school nurses and GPs will continue to see children regularly, both through routine health checks and whenever there are particular health problems. Children who suffer injury or are seriously ill will usually be brought to hospital. Health professionals are therefore generally in the best position to identify children who may be at risk, especially in the period before children start school.

Health professionals who work with children and families, whatever their specialism, therefore need to know the main signs and symptoms that indicate a child may be failing to thrive, suffering from non-accidental injury, sexually abused or otherwise ill-treated. They need to know what to do if they suspect abuse, where to get expert help if they are uncertain, and whom to inform if they have concerns. It is the responsibility of managers and trainers to ensure that all medical staff are equipped to respond to indications that something untoward may be happening which places a child at risk.

A particular problem for some health professionals will be what to do if they find out information relating to a child in the course of treating adult patients. For example, a GP may be told, in confidence, about a child being mistreated, or a patient may admit to a psychiatrist that he or she has been sexually abusing a child. Government and professional bodies (like the GMC) offer guidelines about what course of action must be followed in such situations.

Contributing to investigations

Investigations of child abuse will usually (but not always) involve medical expertise. When a family's circumstances are being examined, the social worker will generally check at an early stage with the family's GP and/or health visitor, who will, in most cases, be able to provide important information not just about medical matters, but also about the family's living conditions, who is living in the household and so on. This may raise issues of confidentiality, so health professionals working in the community will need to be able to refer to agreed guidelines on how this will be handled.

Medical examinations

Where requests are made by social services for medical examinations and other forms of assessment which are part of a joint investigation, health professionals need to know how to respond. In particular, where there is any possibility that the results of the medical examination may be required by a court (including being made available to a Guardian ad Litem [s42]), they should not go ahead until they have informed themselves of the local procedures which apply and the arrangements which have been made locally for such examinations. Non-specialists (e.g. GPs) should always seek advice (for example, from the designated doctor in child protection).

It is important to bear in mind that, where a child is involved in any court proceedings (see chapters 5 and 8), the court may make directions expressly prohibiting or limiting medical examinations. As we have seen, children and young people who are capable of making an informed decision may also refuse to submit to an examination, even where it has been ordered by a court.

Health professionals may also be involved in interviews which are conducted with children for the purposes of an investigation and/or contributing evidence (this may be for child protection proceedings, criminal proceedings or both, see chapter 5 for more details). They may be asked to give expert advice on interviewing children with disabilities or where a child is exhibiting signs of psychiatric disorder. In some cases they may need to be involved in the interview itself, especially where the child has problems in communicating.

Contributing to court proceedings

Health professionals will need to be familiar with the new arrangements for directions appointments (see chapters 2 and 8), whereby information to be put before the court (documentary evidence and summaries of the substance of oral evidence) needs both to be agreed and made available to the court and parties some time before the hearing. The court's powers to set strict timescales will obviously have an impact, and special arrangements may need to be made to comply with them.

Child Assessment and Emergency Protection Orders

Health professionals should familiarise themselves with the particular provisions of these orders (see chapter 5). If they are likely to be asked to contribute to any assessment or examination, they will need to make sure they are in a position to liaise effectively with other agencies in order to be able to comply with the tight deadlines that are set.

Care and Supervision Orders

When a Supervision Order is made or varied (see chapter 8 for more details), it may include directions that a child or young person be medically or psychiatrically examined or treated [Sched 3(4)&(5)]. However, such directions may not be included unless suitable arrangements can be made and supporting medical evidence provided. In such cases, the applicant (a local authority or the NSPCC) will need, before the application is heard in court, to work closely with the medical staff concerned.

With respect to a Care Order, health professionals will often be involved in helping to draw up plans for the child. For example, where a child has suffered sexual abuse, these plans may include a programme of therapy for the child and support for foster carers in looking after the child.

Monitoring

In chapter 5 the investigative process was described. It was noted that, in many cases, an investigation may be inconclusive in its findings. While no definite indications can be found to suggest a child is at risk of significant harm, concerns about the child cannot be fully allayed. In such situations, health professionals will often have an important role to play in monitoring the child's health and development, and alerting the appropriate authorities of any significant changes or new information which emerges.

Treatment and aftercare

As well as specific forms of treatment offered under a Supervision Order or as part of the work done with children in care, specific forms of treatment and aftercare will often play a part in the services provided to children in need. For example, family therapy may be needed as part of the work done with families, following intervention.

8 *Statutory intervention: care and supervision*

While the Children Act legislation explicitly seeks to avoid statutory intervention into the upbringing and care of children and young people, it nonetheless recognises that there will be some cases where it will be necessary for the state to intervene. In chapter 5 we examined short-term intervention for the purposes of immediate protection from harm. In this chapter we will consider legislation concerning long-term intervention. This can take one of two forms:

Supervision: where the local authority does not gain parental responsibility, but is given legal powers to supervise specified aspects of the child's upbringing, care and (possibly) treatment.

Taking the child 'into care': where the local authority gains parental responsibility. While it shares this with the child's parent(s), and the parent(s) retain the right to be consulted and participate in decision-making, the local authority is given a legal obligation to maintain and accommodate the child and the legal authority to direct how, where and by whom the child is looked after and brought up.

In terms of applying to the court and the making of an order, the basic principles are the same. They differ in terms of outcome of course.

CARE AND SUPERVISION PROCEEDINGS

Care and supervision proceedings should only be considered after all reasonable attempts to work in partnership with parents have failed or broken down, and there are sufficient concerns about a child's welfare or safety to require statutory intervention. This may arise following a crisis when the child was removed from a dangerous situation, usually under an Emergency Protection Order (see chapter 5). At other times it could be after a full assessment and then long-term work with a family which fails to bring about sufficient improvement, and where further intervention is being resisted, thwarted or undermined. Whereas other problems (such as truancy) are no longer, in themselves, grounds for making a Care Order, in some instances they may be relevant to a decision about the incidence of harm and its significance. In such circumstances, the local authority or the NSPCC may apply, under section 31 of the Children Act, for a Care or Supervision Order.

*S*UPERVISION ORDER [s31]

Who may apply? The local authority or NSPCC.

Period of notice: The minimum period is three days.

Parties: The child, and every person whom the applicant believes has parental responsibility for the child. A Guardian ad Litem will be appointed to safeguard the child's interests.

Others entitled to notice: includes parents without parental responsibility and any person with whom the child is living or who is providing a refuge.

Welfare checklist: applies, as do the presumption of no order [s1(5)] and paramountcy principle [s1(1)].

Grounds: The court must be satisfied that:

1 the child is suffering or is likely to suffer significant harm; *and*
2 the harm or likelihood of harm is attributable to:
   (a) *either* the care given to the child (or likely to be given if the order were not made), not being what it would be reasonable to expect a parent to give him or her,

(b) *or* the child being beyond parental control.

Powers and duties: The effect of the order is to set up a formal relationship between the child, the 'responsible person' (somebody who has parental responsibility for the child or with whom the child is living) and a 'supervisor' (a social worker or a probation officer). The supervisor is required to advise, assist and befriend the child, give effect to the order, and consider if and when the order may need to be terminated.

The Supervision Order may contain a requirement that the child and the 'responsible person' comply with directions given by the supervisor. These can include where the child is to live and participation in specified activities. The order may also contain requirements about medical and psychiatric examination and treatment.

The child: may, if 'of sufficient understanding to make an informed decision', refuse to submit to medical examination or treatment.

Duration: An interim Supervision Order can initially be made for eight weeks, with extensions of generally up to four weeks. A full Supervision Order lasts for one year, with possible extensions up to a maximum of three years. It cannot be continued after the child's 18th birthday.

Discharge: The Supervision Order can be discharged by the making of a Care Order, or on successful application by the child, parent (or another with parental responsibility) or supervisor.

Challenge: Appeal is to the High Court or Court of Appeal.

CARE ORDER [s31]

Who may apply? The local authority or NSPCC.

Period of notice: The minimum period of notice is three days.

Parties: The child and every person whom the applicant believes to have parental responsibility for the child. A Guardian ad Litem will be appointed to safeguard the child's interests.

Others entitled to notice: includes parents without parental responsibility and any person with whom the child is living or who is providing a refuge.

Welfare checklist: applies, as do the presumption of no order [s1(5)] and paramountcy principle [s1(1)].

Grounds: The court must be satisfied that:

1 the child is suffering or is likely to suffer significant harm; *and*
2 that the harm or likelihood of harm is attributable to:
   (a) *either* the care given to the child (or likely to be given if the order were not made) not being what it would be reasonable to expect a parent to give him or her,
   (b) *or* the child being beyond parental control.

Powers and duties: The local authority is placed under a duty to receive the child into its care and keep him or her in care while the order remains in force. This includes providing accommodation for and maintaining the child.

The local authority acquires parental responsibility for the child, which it shares with the parents. However, it can determine the extent to which a parent or guardian may meet his or her parental responsibility, in order to safeguard the child's welfare.

For specific duties see section 23(6)–(9) and Schedule 2, part II. For specific restrictions on the local authority's powers, see section 33(5)–(9). There is a presumption of reasonable contact between the child and parents, guardians, anybody who held a Residence Order with respect to the child, and any person who (before the order was made) had the care of the child under the inherent jurisdiction of the High Court.

Duration: An interim Care Order can initially be made for eight weeks, with extensions of generally up to four weeks. A full Care Order lasts until the child's 18th birthday, unless it is brought to an end earlier.

Discharge: The Care Order can be discharged by adoption, the making of a Residence or Supervision Order, or on application by the child, the local authority or anyone with parental responsibility for the child.

Challenge: Appeal is to the High Court or Court of Appeal.

The basis on which a Care or Supervision Order can be made

A further change introduced by the Act is that, for the court to make an order, a two-stage process of decision-making must be followed.

Meeting the threshold criteria
An order cannot be justified merely because the court believes that a particular child would be better off living somewhere else other than with his or her parents. The question is not 'where will the child's welfare be best safeguarded and promoted?'. Rather, the issues at stake are 'is the child at risk of significant harm?' and 'is this harm attributable to some failing in the care provided by the child's parents?' In the passage of the Bill through the Lords, the Lord Chancellor explained that 'unless there is evidence that a child is being or is likely to be positively

harmed because of a failure in the family, the state, whether in the guise of a local authority or the court, should not interfere'.

The grounds to be proved, as set out in section 31(2), are known as the *threshold criteria* for making a Care or Supervision Order. This is because they are the *minimum* circumstances that would justify compulsory intervention into family life. Unless these are proved, neither a Care nor a Supervision Order can be made, although another order (e.g. a Residence Order) can.

Meeting the section 1 principles

Even where the threshold criteria are established, the Act's section 1 principles must also be satisfied. The result of this is that once the section 31(2) 'threshold' is crossed, the court will treat the welfare of the child as the paramount consideration. It is required to consider all the elements of the welfare checklist [s1(3)] and, in particular, will be required not to make an order 'unless it considers that doing so would be better for the child than making no order at all' [s1(5)]. Even if the court does decide to make an order, it will not necessarily be the order applied for – this is because proceedings for a Care or Supervision Order are 'family proceedings' and in such proceedings the court can make any of the section 8 orders or a 'Family Assistance Order' (see chapter 3).

Thus the decision-making process must proceed through a specified and systematic route. This is shown in Figure 8.1.

Satisfying the threshold criteria

The threshold criteria [s31(2)] are that:

1   the child is suffering or is likely to suffer significant harm; *and*
2   that the harm, or likelihood of harm is attributable to:
    (a)   *either* the care given to the child (or likely to be given if the order were not made) not being what it would be reasonable to expect a parent to give him or her,
    (b)   *or* the child being beyond parental control.

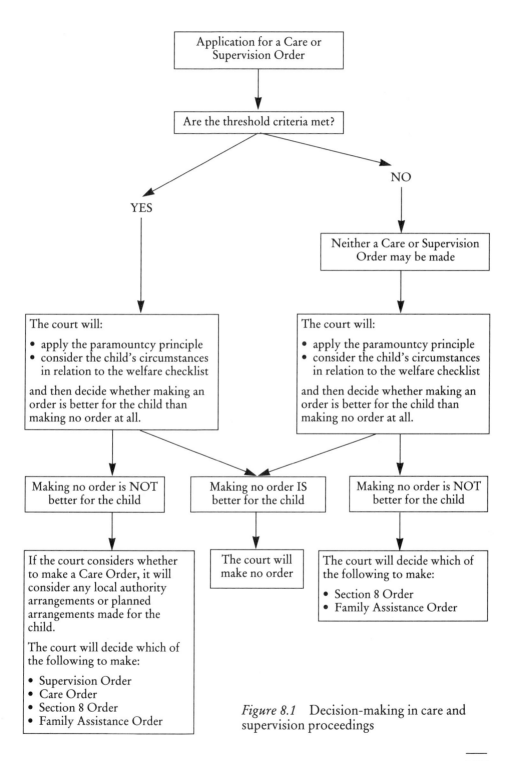

Figure 8.1 Decision-making in care and supervision proceedings

In order to see how these apply, it is necessary to consider the meaning of three phrases in the section:

- 'significant harm'
- 'likely to suffer'
- 'attributable to'

Significant harm

The Guidance (Volume 1) refers first to harm and then to the question of its significance. On the question of *harm* it states '"Harm" is defined in section 31(9) as ill-treatment or the impairment of health or development' [Vol 1, para 3.19]. It is important to note that these are alternatives. On the question of the meaning of *significant* it states:

> *Having set an acceptable standard of upbringing for the child, it is necessary to show some significant deficit in that standard. Minor shortcomings in health care or minor deficits in physical, psychological or social development should not require compulsory intervention unless cumulatively they are having, or are likely to have, serious and lasting effects upon the child.*
> [Vol 1, para 3.21]

If there are only 'minor shortcomings', the local authority will be expected to provide appropriate services for the child and family so as to comply with their statutory duty, under section 17, to promote the upbringing of children in their own families. Whether harm is significant or not is, in general terms, a question for the court to decide – no further guidance is given on this, since the idea is to give courts discretion to make judgements case by case, according to circumstances. However, where the question of whether harm suffered by a child is significant depends on the child's health or development, the child's health or development must be compared with that which could reasonably be expected of a similar child [s31(10)].

During the debates in Parliament, it was stated that the phrase 'a similar child' referred to children's physical attributes and not their social background. However, it is arguable that the phrase can be interpreted so as to include wider social and environmental factors. In the case of **Re O** [1992] 2 FLR 7 (a case involving truancy), the court stated that the phrase 'similar child' referred to 'a child of equivalent intellectual and social development who has gone to school, and not merely an average child who may or may not be at school'. This case is of interest for another reason – it illustrates that persistent truancy can bring a child within the wording of section 31(2).

Likely to suffer

This phrasing now makes it possible to work on the basis of anticipated harm in the future. The wording of the Act makes this explicit, though some observations in earlier cases are important. In particular, in the case of **M v Westminster C.C.** [1985] FLR 325, the court stated:

> *A child's development is a continuing process. The present must be relevant in the context of what has happened in the past, and it becomes a matter of degree as to how far in the past you go.*

The Act, having settled this question, has provoked another. How does the court determine the question of the *likelihood* of harm – simply on the basis of the standard of proof in civil proceedings (i.e. the balance of probabilities)? In the case of **Newham LBC v AG** [1993] 1 FLR 281, the court said not. The Court of Appeal stated:

> *The court is not applying a test to events which have happened in the past and deciding on the evidence, on the balance of probabilities, which is the standard of civil proof, whether such an event has in fact happened. That is not what is involved in this case. … The court has to be satisfied that the child concerned is suffering or is likely to suffer significant harm, but in looking to the future the court has to assess the risk. Is this child likely to suffer significant harm? … The Judge had to make an assessment of the future risk in the light of the evidence before him. That is entirely a matter for the Judge. It is the duty which he has to discharge in the exercise of his discretion.*

Attributable to

Not only must the court be satisfied that the significant harm test is made out, it must also be satisfied that this harm, or its likelihood, is 'attributable to' a deficiency in parental care. This requirement is linked either to the care being given to the child 'not being what it would be reasonable to expect a parent to give' or 'the child's being beyond parental control'. The question is, what is reasonable to expect a parent to provide? The test is objective. That is, it is not asking what it is reasonable to expect *this* parent to provide, but *a* parent to provide for this child. The hypothetical parent would be a reasonable parent. Guidance states:

> *The actual parents may be doing their best, but are not able to meet the child's particular needs and are unwilling or incapable of making use of appropriate services.... The court must compare the care being given to the child in question with what it would be reasonable to expect a reasonable parent to give him, having regard to his needs.*
> [Vol 1, para 3.23]

So, it is clear that the court must take into account any special needs which the child may have and consider whether these parents are providing the standard of care that reasonable parents would do, in order to meet those needs.

BOX 8.1 WHAT MUST BE CONSIDERED BEFORE APPLYING FOR A CARE ORDER?

Guidance [Vol 1, para 3.12] advises that, before applying for a Care Order, local authorities should seek legal advice (preferably within the context of the multi-agency child protection conference) on:

1   whether, in the circumstances of the case and having regard to the welfare checklist, the court is likely to be satisfied that the 'threshold criteria' [s31(2)] are satisfied;

2   whether, in the circumstances of the case, the court is likely to be satisfied that making an order will be better for the child than making no order at all [s1(5)];

3   the implications of another party to the proceedings (e.g. a relative of the child) opposing the application and applying for a section 8 order instead;

4   whether the application falls within criteria of transfer of cases, and whether representations about this should be made;

5   whether the court should be asked for an interim Care or Supervision Order, what is the desired length of the initial order, and what directions should be sought.

6   what needs to be provided for in the authority's advance statement of the case, including copies of witness statements and an outline of the authority's plans for the child.

7   whether a Residence Order with respect to a relative, linked with a Supervision Order would be an appropriate alternative to a Care Order.

Interim orders

Under the old law there was a power to make an interim Care Order but not an interim Supervision Order. Now both can be made and directions given as to medical and psychiatric examinations and assessments.

Where an Emergency Protection Order has been made to protect a child from immediate danger, this lasts for eight days. Even allowing for an extension of the order for a further seven days, it would usually take much longer for the child's circumstances to be investigated and a case to be prepared for care or supervision proceedings. In these circumstances, a local authority will usually apply to the court for an order, but request an interim Care Order. All the authority needs to do in this situation is to satisfy the court that there are reasonable grounds for believing that the conditions necessary for a full Care Order apply. Further time will allow evidence about these to be presented to the court. The interim Care Order gives the local authority the powers it needs to protect the child and, at the same time, to conduct an investigation to gather information for a full hearing.

BOX 8.2 GUIDELINES FOR INTERIM CARE ORDERS

In the recent case of **Hampshire C.C. v S** [1993] 1 FLR 559, the court issued guidelines for the courts hearing such applications:

1   An interim order is a holding order, but the court should nevertheless consider all relevant risks pending the substantive hearing and should ensure (perhaps by giving directions) that the final hearing takes place at the earliest possible date.

2   The courts should be prepared to transfer the case laterally if time is not available.

3   Courts should be cautious about changing a child's residence on an interim order.

4   Where an interim order would lead to a substantial change in the child's position, then the court should permit the hearing of limited evidence, but must ensure that there is not a dress rehearsal of the full hearing.

5   The court should ensure that it has the written advice of the Guardian ad Litem. Any party opposed to the Guardian ad Litem's advice should be given an opportunity to put questions.

6   When granting an interim order, justices should state their findings and reasons concisely and summarise briefly the essential factual issues between the parties. The justices will not, however, be able to make findings as to the facts where evidence is disputed.

There is one circumstance when the court is under a duty to make an interim Supervision Order – that is when, on an application for a Care or Supervision Order, the court makes a Residence Order. In this case, it must also make an interim Supervision Order, unless it is satisfied that the child's welfare will be satisfactorily safeguarded without an interim order being made [s38(3)]. There are two situations where the court might make a Residence Order in such proceedings: where it is not yet in a position to make a final order and makes a Residence Order as an interim measure, and as a final decision in the case.

Duration of interim orders

On the question of the duration of interim orders and the number of such orders, the Guidance states:

> *Although there is no limit to the number of orders that can be made under the Act, a balance will have to be struck between allowing sufficient time for enquiries, reports and statements, and risking allowing the child to continue in interim care or supervision for so long that the balance of advantage is distorted in favour of continued intervention.*
> [Vol 1, para 3.46]

Interim orders can be as short as the court considers appropriate. As a general rule, no interim order can last for more than four weeks. However, there is an initial eight-week period, beginning on the day on which the court makes an interim order for the first time. Provided the interim order does not exceed this eight-week period, the order can be of any length. This eight-week period could consist of a single interim order lasting eight weeks or a series of shorter orders of varying duration lasting a total of eight weeks (e.g. one week, one week and then six weeks). If, towards the end of this eight-week period, a court wishes to make an interim order which would overrun the period, then the general 'four-week rule' would apply for the order, and for any subsequent order sought.

COURT PROCEEDINGS

In this section, we will examine briefly the main features of care and supervision proceedings, once they come to court.

Applications

Almost all applications for Care and Supervision Orders are made to the Magistrates' Court. The relevant Rules are the Family Proceedings Court (Children Act 1989) Rules.

Application forms

The application form, Form CHA 19, is set out in Schedule 1 of the Rules of Court. This is comprehensive, covering information about: the child, the applicant and the family; directions, parental responsibility and any other concurrent applications concerning the child; the grounds for the application and reasons why it is believed these are satisfied; and the local authority's (or NSPCC's) plans for the child if the order is made. Copies of the form must be made available to all parties to the proceedings, in good time, so that all concerned are pre-appraised of the exact issues at stake at the hearing.

Allocation to a court

The Children (Allocation of Proceedings) Order 1991 (included in Volume 7 of *Guidance and Regulations*) specifies that care and supervision proceedings should usually be started and heard in the Magistrates' Court, although they can be transferred if circumstances demand this (see chapter 2). An exception is where a High Court or County Court has directed that a local authority should investigate the child's circumstances, or where other public law proceedings with respect to the child are pending in higher courts. In such cases, only specified judges will be able to hear the case.

Participation in proceedings

In care and supervision proceedings, the respondents (the child and all those believed to have parental responsibility) are full parties to the proceedings and, as such, are entitled to be legally represented, call evidence, cross-examine witnesses and appeal a decision. Anyone caring for the child at the time when proceedings are commenced, any unmarried father without parental responsibility, and anyone party to other Children Act proceedings with respect to the child are entitled to receive notice of the proceedings and may apply to become a party. Others (such as relatives) may also apply for party status. (For the availability of legal aid, see glossary.)

The directions appointment

Prior to the hearing proper there will usually be a directions appointment (see chapter 2) at which arrangements will be made about timetabling, whether the child should attend, and what information and reports will need to be submitted. If a Guardian ad Litem has not been appointed already, arrangements will be made for appointment. Other matters that may be considered are transfer of the case and consolidation with other proceedings. The rules require the court to arrange a timetable for the proceedings and, if they are postponed or adjourned, the court must fix a date for another hearing. If at the directions appointment the applicant tells the court that they are applying for an interim order, they must state what plans have been made for protecting the child and for the child's contact with his or her parents and others while it is in force.

Evidence

A number of significant changes have been introduced with respect to the evidence which is admissible in family proceedings and how it is to be dealt with by the court.

Admissibility of evidence

The Children (Admissibility of Hearsay Evidence) Order 1991 specifies that in family proceedings 'evidence given in connection with the upbringing, maintenance or welfare of a child shall be admissible, notwithstanding any rule of law relating to hearsay'. What this means, in effect, is that in care and supervision proceedings, the usual rules of hearsay do not apply (see chapter 2) and the court can consider second-hand accounts of events. For example, a teacher can tell the court about allegations a child has made to him or her, and it is admissible for the court to take account of what is said (unlike in criminal proceedings, where such an account would be hearsay). Similarly, any relevant statement in the Guardian ad Litem's report can be considered [s41(11)], as can official records examined by the Guardian [s42(2)].

Medical examinations

Concerns were raised, particularly in the aftermath of the events in Cleveland, about exposing children to repeated medical examinations for the purposes of evidence. Consequently, the Children Act directs that courts can set conditions (e.g. when making interim orders) to limit the conducting of medical examinations. In addition, the rules of court expressly prevent anyone (whether the applicant or respondents in the case) having the child medically or psychiatrically examined for the preparation of expert evidence for use in the proceedings, without the court's permission.

Advance disclosure of evidence

Each of the parties to the proceedings is required to file with the court, and serve on the other parties, written statements of the substance of the oral evidence and copies of any documents (including experts' reports) which they intend to submit when the case is heard. At the directions appointment, a major task will be establishing the evidence, making arrangements for its submission to the court and prior disclosure to other parties. It should also seek to resolve those issues not in dispute, and to identify the key areas at issue on which the case will hang. The aim is to clarify, for all concerned, what will be at stake and to reduce the need to cover unnecessary ground in the proceedings about those aspects of the case which are not at issue.

An important purpose of these provisions is to prevent one of the parties from springing new evidence on other parties once the case comes to court. While the rules do not entirely prohibit the introduction of new evidence at the hearing, this is seen to be only acceptable in exceptional circumstances, and then only when the court has given permission for it to be brought.

Hearing the case

Given that cases may vary so much, with an almost infinite permutation of parties being able to present and argue a case and with the court able to make a diverse range of orders, it is impossible to neatly summarise what course the 'typical' case will take in court. All we can do here is set out the main thrust of what will happen.

Prior to the hearing

Prior to the hearing itself, the magistrates or judge will have had an opportunity to review all the written information – both the documents to be considered and written summaries of the oral evidence to be presented. They are likely to have done a fair amount of thinking about the merits of the various outcomes that are being suggested by the different parties, including the Guardian ad Litem's report. In this process they will often identify particular issues they wish to have clarified and alternative options they would like to consider.

At the hearing itself

At the hearing itself the parties will, in turn, present their case and bring their evidence. Once each of them has done this, they can be cross-examined by or on behalf of the other parties and can be questioned by the magistrates or the judge. Thus the main body of the hearing will consist of a sequence of parties arguing and defending their case in turn.

Considering the threshold criteria

The magistrates or judge will then retire to consider the evidence put before them. In the case of magistrates, they will be advised by the Justices' Clerk. At this point, following the two-step decision-making framework set out in the legislation, they will first consider whether the 'threshold criteria' have been satisfied – whether there are grounds for making a Care or Supervision Order. To do this, they evaluate just the evidence relevant to these grounds *alone* and make 'findings of fact' about them (i.e. decide whether or not there is sufficient convincing evidence to satisfy them that each element of the threshold criteria is met). They will note these in writing.

If the threshold criteria are not satisfied, then the judge or magistrates cannot make a Care or Supervision Order. They will then consider whether to make any order at all, in the light of the section 1 principles. To do this they will look at the other evidence that has been presented – for example, any suggestions made in the Guardian's report about an alternative order. If they do decide that making an order is better for the child than making no order at all, they can make another order at this stage. For example, they could make a Residence Order with respect to the child's grandparents (see Figure 8.1, page 157).

Considering the child's welfare

Where the court is satisfied that its findings of fact indicate that the threshold criteria are met, it will then go on to consider the other parts of the evidence – such as the local authority's plans for the child. Again, the judge or magistrates will need to consider whether to make any order at all. If they do decide to make an order, they can make a Supervision or Care Order, but they can, alternatively, make another order (e.g. a Residence Order), notwithstanding their finding that the threshold criteria are satisfied.

Announcing the decision

Whatever the decision made, the judge or magistrates will return to the courtroom, where the parties will be re-assembled, and announce their decision. The Rules of Court specify that they must inform the parties of their findings of fact, the reasons for them, the decisions they have made (including any directions made within orders) and the reasons why they have made them. These must be noted in writing and copies supplied to all parties to the proceedings.

THE EFFECTS OF CARE AND SUPERVISION ORDERS

We will now consider, in more detail, how these orders operate in practice.

The effects of a Supervision Order

A Supervision Order does not grant parental responsibility to the local authority. Rather, it provides a form of statutory intervention whereby a child's welfare and safety can be closely monitored and services provided to help overcome the problems that the child is experiencing. The effect of the order is to set up a formal, agreed relationship between three classes of people:

- the supervisor;
- the supervised child;
- the responsible person.

The *responsible person* is defined in the Act as any person who has parental responsibility for the child, or any person with whom the child is living who has agreed to act in this capacity and (thereby) to comply with the requirements of the Supervision Order [Sched 3, para 3]. The supervisor will generally be a social worker but can, in some cases, be a probation officer. Details of the order are provided in Schedule 3 of the Act.

The authority and duties of the supervisor

The Act requires the supervisor to advise, assist and befriend the child, to give effect to the order, and to consider whether to apply to the court for variation or discharge. Supervisors are empowered to require the responsible person and the supervised child to comply with their directions about such things as where the child is to live or that he or she will attend a family centre. They must also be kept informed of the child's address and be allowed to visit the child. However, supervisors do not have the power to do things like make the child attend for medical treatment or examinations – only the court can make such requirements. Usually the requirements will be quite specific. For example, the court may order that a particular doctor carry out an examination or that medical treatment is to be provided in a particular clinic.

The effects of a Care Order

Once a child is placed 'in care' the local authority acquires parental responsibility and the power to determine the extent to which those with parental responsibility for the child may meet this responsibility [s33(3)]. In effect, this means that the local authority has a great deal of discretion in deciding matters concerning the child's upbringing and what role the parents will play.

Limits on what the local authority may do

Local authorities will never, however, have a completely free hand with regard to children in their care. There are some specific exclusions to their authority [s33(6)]. While a child is in their care the local authority cannot:

- cause the child to be brought up in any religious persuasion other than that in which he or she would have been brought up if the order had not been made;
- consent or refuse to consent to the making of an application that the child be freed for adoption, or agree or refuse to agree to the making of an Adoption Order;
- appoint a guardian for the child.
- cause the child to be known by a new surname without either the consent of all persons with parental responsibility or the permission of the court.
- remove the child from the UK for a month or longer, without either the written consent of every person who has parental responsibility for the child or the permission of the court.

Arranging for the child to live outside of England and Wales

Special arrangements apply when a local authority decides that a child should live somewhere outside of England and Wales (see Box 8.3). Such a situation might arise, for example, if a child had settled in foster care and the foster-parents were moving to live in Germany.

BOX 8.3	ARRANGING FOR A CHILD 'IN CARE' TO LIVE OUTSIDE ENGLAND AND WALES

Before a local authority can arrange or assist in arranging for any child in their care to live outside England and Wales, they must obtain the leave of the court [Sched 2(19)(3)]. The court is not to give its approval unless it is satisfied that:

1 living outside England and Wales would be in the child's best interests;

2 suitable arrangements have been, or will be, made for the child's reception and welfare in the country in which he or she will live;

3 the child, if of sufficient understanding to make the decision, has consented to living in that country;

4 every person who has parental responsibility consents to the child living in that country. This can be dispensed with if they cannot be

found, are incapable of consenting, or are withholding their consent unreasonably.

It is quite clear from the Guidance [Vol 8] that such a move is viewed as a serious matter with the potential to cause severe disruption in the life of the child concerned. It states:

> *There are profound implications for those involved in a move abroad, but particularly so for the child. Careful consideration needs to be given to the balance to be struck between gaining a settled family life against the loss of familiar people and surroundings.*
> [*Guidance*, Vol 8, para 4.8]

Marriage in care

If a child who is in care wants to marry, they must obtain the consent of each parent with parental responsibility and the designated local authority. However, if any required consent is not given, the young person in care can apply to court – its consent will be an effective substitute for the withheld consent.

Duty to consult

In addition to all these constraints, local authorities are under a duty to consult the child, the child's parents and any others with parental responsibility about the arrangements to be made for the child's upbringing. They will also have had to provide the court with information about their plans as part of the care proceedings and, in broad terms, will be expected to follow those plans. Any significant deviations should be negotiated with the child and parents.

Placing the child

When applying for Care Orders, local authorities will need to conduct comprehensive assessments of each child's circumstances and needs, and make plans for their placement. Factors which need to be taken into account when finding an appropriate placement for a child will therefore vary considerably from case to case. There are some general principles (see Box 8.4). Placement with the child's own family should be considered first (this is covered in more detail later in this chapter). Next, the possibility of placement with the child's extended family or others with whom the child is familiar should be explored. Only if neither of these options are viable should placement elsewhere be considered. The child and parents must be consulted and their wishes taken into account. Placements should generally be within the child's own community, as close to home as possible and where, for example, the child can continue at the same school.

BOX 8.4	PRINCIPLES TO BE CONSIDERED WHEN PLACING A CHILD

These are set out in *Guidance and Regulations* [Vol 3, para 5. 22]. The following aspects need to be considered:

Ease of contact with family: includes siblings and other relatives. This is particularly important when, for example, the child's foster-parent is not of the same racial or cultural group as the child.

Health-care needs: children with disabilities may need specialist care and the carer may need to acquire knowledge and skills to cope with a child's medical condition.

Education: continuity will be especially important if the child is at a critical stage in his or her education.

Religion: if this is important in the life of the child and his or her family, it *must* be addressed. It must not be assumed that both parents are of the same religion, or the child has the same religion as the parent(s). Foster parents should be of the same religious persuasion as the child or willing to give an undertaking that the child will be brought up in that religious persuasion.

Race, culture and linguistic needs: the Guidance states that 'in seeking to understand fully a child's needs and considering the suitability of a placement, social workers need to be aware of differences between minority groups and the significance of religion and culture in relation to racial origin, and to guard against simplistic assumptions of similarity. … As an important principle, children should be given opportunities and encouragement to enjoy and take pride in their racial and cultural heritage.'

Needs of siblings: these are central, though the needs of the child in care should not be subordinated to the needs of the siblings as a group.

Support: this must be considered and may take a number of forms, including the involvement of voluntary organisations. Examples given are a family aide, day care or the provision of essential household items.

Protection: local authorities must check their records and liaise with the police and other agencies as appropriate, to make sure the child will be safe.

Standards: there should be at least one visit to the placement during which the social worker can meet the *entire* household and see the relationships within it. The proposed accommodation for the child must also be checked. Accommodation for children with disabilities must not be unsuitable for their needs.

Contact between child and family

Local authorities are required to promote contact between the child and family unless this is not reasonably practicable or consistent with the child's welfare [Sched 2, para 15]. Section 34 of the Act imposes a positive duty on local authorities to allow such children contact with their parents and other specified persons. Where there are disputes which cannot be settled by agreement, it is the court which has the power to make orders concerning contact. These are called section 34 Contact Orders (to differentiate them from the section 8 Contact Order).

SECTION 34 CONTACT ORDER [s34]

Who may apply? As of right, the child or the local authority; the child's parent (including the unmarried father) or guardian; a person in whose favour a Residence Order existed prior to the making of the Care Order; and any person who had care of the child immediately before the making of the Care Order by virtue of an order of the High Court under its inherent jurisdiction. Other people (e.g. relatives) may apply with the leave of the court. Only the local authority or the child can apply for contact to be *refused*.

Period of notice: three days

Parties: includes all those whom the applicant believes to have parental responsibility for the child, the local authority, the child him or herself, and any person whose contact with the child is the subject of the application. A Guardian ad Litem will be appointed to safeguard the child's interests.

Others entitled to notice: includes any person with whom the child is living or who is providing a refuge.

Welfare checklist: applies, as do the presumption of no order [s1(5)] and paramountcy principle [s1(1)].

Grounds: The welfare of the child is the paramount consideration. There is a presumption that the child is entitled to contact with all those entitled to apply for it. When making a Care Order, the court must consider the arrangements for contact that the local authority has made or proposes making. The court may make a section 34 Contact Order, even though no application for the order has been made.

Powers and duties: The order will specify with whom the child should have contact, and can impose such conditions as it considers appropriate.

Duration: The order lasts until the child reaches the age of eighteen or as specified in the order.

Variation: The child, the local authority or the person(s) named in the order can apply for its variation or discharge. It ceases to apply once the child is no longer in care.

Challenge: Appeal is to the High Court or Court of Appeal. If contact is refused, the applicant cannot re-apply for six months, unless given leave by the court.

– CHRISTINE'S STORY –

Christine is nine years old. Following concerns raised by her teacher that she had made allegations against her father of sexual assault, the local authority investigated her case. They interviewed Christine, who told them that her father had been forcing her to have intercourse with him for two years. An Emergency Protection Order was made and Christine went to live with foster-parents. Care proceedings followed, as well as criminal proceedings. A Care Order was made. However, criminal proceedings against the father failed, as Christine broke down under cross-examination and the forensic evidence was not sufficient to prove that it was her father who had assaulted her.

Christine has had regular contact with her mother, which has proved very difficult. Her mother shows considerable hostility towards her daughter and refuses to believe Christine's accusations about her father. Both parents now claim that he has been 'shown to be innocent'. Christine's father makes an application for contact. Christine has said she does not want to have anything more to do with him and never wants to see him again. She has also, recently, begun to say she does not want to go on seeing her mother. The local authority decide that contact between Christine and her parents should be terminated.

The local authority cannot just decide to terminate contact between Christine and her parents. If they wish to do so, they must apply to the court [s34(4)]. In the short-term they can refuse to allow contact for a maximum of seven days, but only if they are satisfied this is necessary to safeguard or promote Christine's welfare and the refusal is decided upon as a matter of urgency [s34(6)]. In court proceedings, the welfare checklist will be considered. In this case, Christine's wishes are likely to be an important factor.

Disputes between parents and the local authority

The spirit of the Act is that all those involved with children in care must co-operate to the best of their ability, in order to promote the interests of the child concerned. Even when a child is in care, the obligation to work in partnership with parents does not cease. This is expressed in the ways in which the Act promotes continued contact with and involvement of parents in relation to children in care. The Guidance refers to the intention underpinning the Children Act [Vol 3, para 2.3]:

> *that parents should be encouraged to exercise their responsibility for their child's welfare in a constructive way and that where compulsory intervention is used it should, where possible, enhance rather than undermine the parental role.*

Local authorities must regularly hold reviews for the children they are looking after, at which parents will usually attend. They must also operate a complaints procedure with an independent element in it (see chapter 9 for more details). However, once parents have made their views known through the review process and/or made a complaint, if these fail and if they are unhappy with what the local authority is doing, they can apply for the discharge of the Care Order. Alternatively it is possible for them to apply for a variation of contact under section 34 – using this, in effect, as a device to bring their concerns to the attention of the court.

PERMANENCY PLANNING

When a child is placed in care, especially where younger children are concerned, the local authority is expected to take steps to offer the child a stable future. This can be achieved in a number of ways. First, attempts can be made to return the child home with his or her family. This is regarded as the most desirable option – other possibilities should not be explored until or unless this proves to be impossible to achieve and still safeguard the child's welfare. Secondly, a secure, long-term placement can be found for the child with foster-parents. Thirdly, the child may be placed for adoption. Finally, especially where older children are concerned, some young people themselves may prefer to live in a hostel or children's home and this option needs to be made available to them as a positive choice.

Returning the child home

When a child is taken into care, the expectation is that the child should be returned home as soon as possible, so long as this will be consistent with safeguarding the child's welfare. When local authorities place children with their own families, the *Placement of Children with Parents Regulations* apply. Inevitably, placing a child back with his or her family will be difficult, in that parents will have day-to-day care of the child while, at the same time, their ability to exercise parental responsibility will be limited. Making such an arrangement work, in practice, will require immense tact and skill from all concerned and a genuine commitment on behalf of the parents to work in partnership.

If this level of co-operation proves to be feasible, it will raise the question as to whether the Care Order is strictly necessary. Indeed, Guidance states that local authorities 'should consider carefully whether a placement under these Regulations is the only way to achieve placing the child with a parent or a person who has or has had parental responsibility' [Vol 3, para 5.2]. It points out that, if placement at home is in the child's best interests, then the local authority may need to consider whether a Care Order is still needed. It continues:

> *In many cases where it is decided that a placement under these regulations is the right approach, it will be seen as part of the progress towards discharge of the Care Order. The management of the placement should aim to enhance the parent's role and support the family relationship with that aim in mind. Even in those cases where the discharge of the Care Order is not a foreseeable option, the possibility should be constantly reviewed and the aim should be to build a genuine working partnership with the parent.*
> [Vol 3, para 5.3]

When the Regulations apply

The Regulations apply when any child in care is placed for more than 24 hours with a parent (or someone who has, or has had immediately prior to the Care Order being made, parental responsibility for the child). If, however, the child in care is aged sixteen or over, then only some of these regulations apply:

- The local authority must satisfy itself that the placement is the most suitable way of complying with their duty under section 22(3) of the Act and that, in all the circumstances, it is suitable [Reg 4];
- The placement decision can only be made by the Director of Social Services or someone nominated by the Director in writing [Reg 5];
- If the placement is outside of England and Wales, the local authority must 'so far as is reasonably practicable' take steps to ensure that the requirements in these regulations are complied with [Reg 10];
- If the placement appears to be no longer suitable they must terminate it and remove the child forthwith [Reg 11].

However, the Guidance goes on to advise local authorities that they will 'wish to consider how far to apply the principles of the other Regulations in their arrangements for such cases, depending on the maturity of the child and the individual circumstances' [Vol 3, para 5.9].

Placement at home at times of crisis

There may be circumstances where such a placement is necessary (e.g. the unforeseen breakdown of a foster placement). In this situation, all the Regulations apply, but Regulation 6 provides that the following checks must be made by the local authority *before* the placement:

- The parent must be interviewed;
- The accommodation must be inspected;
- Information about other persons living in the same household must be obtained.

Again, this placement decision must be made by the Director of Social Services or nominated person. All the other Regulations must be complied with as soon after the placement as possible.

Arrangements to be made

Under these Regulations, any placement requires the local authority to reach agreement on a number of matters with the person with whom the child is to be placed. These include:

- the local authority's plans for the child and the objectives of the placement;
- arrangements for supporting the child and family;
- arrangements for supervising the placement;
- the need to notify the local authority of relevant changes in circumstances;
- a statement of the child's health, any particular health, educational or other needs the child may have, and how these are to be met.

Planned return home

When a planned return home is being considered, all agencies (e.g. the child's school) and individuals (e.g. parents) who are important in the child's life must be consulted, including any statutory and voluntary agencies which have been involved with the child and family. Consultation with the child or young person is especially important. Efforts must be made to find out the wishes of younger as well as older children, and social workers must be alert to the possibility that the child holds quite different views from the parents. The more mature the child, the more his or her wishes must be taken into account.

As always, the stress is on proper planning as one way of reducing the risk of harm to the child. Such a placement must have clear aims and objectives, probably set out in a written agreement. Support (in a variety of forms) will often be needed to help make the placement work. Careful monitoring must be undertaken, with frequent visits to see how the placement is working out, and written records kept.

Adoption

The Children Act did not radically change the law regarding adoption, although it repealed some parts and made amendments to others. At the time of writing, the relevant legislation is the Adoption Act 1976, although major legislative change is underway. We do not have the space to cover this complex and changing area of law in this book, and any person involved in adoption will need to seek specialist advice. All we can do here is to summarise the main points.

Adoption arranged by a local authority, as a consequence of a decision that this offers a child in care the best (or least harmful) option for a settled future, involves both internal agency procedures and court proceedings.

Freeing application

A freeing application can be made irrespective of whether or not there are any prospective adoptive parents in mind. Unless the child's parents agree to its making, as a result of the Children Act it can only be applied for by a local authority with respect to a child for whom they have a Care Order. Application is made to the court, who may make the order even if all the parent(s) and other relevant people (see chapter 3) do not consent, if certain grounds are satisfied. These are where the parent cannot be found; is incapable of giving agreement; is withholding consent unreasonably; has persistently failed to discharge parental responsibility; has abandoned or neglected the child; or has persistently or seriously ill-treated the child. A freeing order is not necessary but, in vesting authority to agree to the adoption with the local authority, it avoids confrontation later in court between the child's birth parent(s) and the prospective adoptive parents.

Satisfying the adoption panel

All local authorities are automatically adoption agencies, and are required to set up an adoption panel, whose task is to review planned adoptions in the initial stage. The first step of the process is that the panel's review procedure must be satisfied by supplying the panel with information about the child's circumstances, why adoption is seen as the best option for the child's future, and about the prospective adoptive parents. The panel will also need to be told if the parent(s) agree to the adoption or not and whether a freeing order has been obtained.

Adoption proceedings

Where an adoption follows a freeing order, the local authority and the potential adoptive parents will be the parties. Where freeing is not involved, the child's birth parents will also be parties. This will usually happen only if parental consent has been given. The adoption can, however, be made without parental consent on similar grounds to the freeing order.

The Adoption Contact Register

The Children Act has provided for the setting up of an Adoption Contact Register to allow people who have been adopted and their birth parents (and other relations) to get in touch with each other. The Register is in two parts. Part 1 contains the names and addresses (and other details relating to the birth) of adoptees who want to get in contact with their parents and/or relatives. Part 2 contains equivalent information from the birth parents or relatives who want to get in contact with adoptees. The Register is administered by the Registrar General (see addresses at the end of this book).

Transfer of parental responsibility

As discussed in chapter 3, local authority foster-parents may apply for a Residence Order. If they are or have been the child's foster-parents in the last six months, and are relatives of the child or have the local authority's permission, they can seek leave to apply for a Residence Order at any time. If the child has lived with them for at least three years (this need not be continuous, but must not have begun more than five years before the application), they may apply without the consent of the local authority (although, of course, the court will want to consider why the local authority has not given its consent). A Residence Order, if made, will give the foster-parents parental responsibility for the child and discharge the Care Order. Others may also apply for a Residence Order (see chapter 3). Thus another alternative is for a relative to take on parental responsibility, by way of a Residence Order being made in his or her favour.

This is an important means, therefore, of providing children with long-term security, while allowing their parents continued involvement in their lives (since they will retain parental responsibility). It may well be more feasible to negotiate than adoption in some cases, given that the child's parents are less likely to feel they are having their child taken away from them, and are assured of continued involvement, the right to be consulted, and so on. It also has the advantage that the child will no longer be 'in care', which some parents find very stigmatising.

Long-term placements

Particularly where teenagers are concerned, the general principle that a family *inherently* offers a better place to live can be challenged. Some young people in care have been highly critical of those local authorities who closed all their hostels and children's homes, and therefore did not offer these as alternatives. They have argued that, for them, this kind of accommodation offers positive benefits, especially when they have suffered a series of foster-placement breakdowns, or where they find this kind of care is easier to cope with in terms of avoiding conflicts with their birth families.

For some children and young people, other forms of residential care may be more appropriate. These include therapeutic communities, boarding schools and homes with education on the premises. In every case, however, the choice of this form of residential care must be made on the basis of the child's or young person's needs. It must be a positive choice, in which the youngster has been offered the opportunity to participate. In the next chapter we examine the legislative framework for children and young people living away from home, including those who are in care.

9 *Children and young people living away from home*

Children and young people can live away from home for a number of quite different reasons and in a range of different kinds of places. As we have seen already, some do so because they are 'looked after' by a local authority, either because they are being provided with accommodation (as described in chapter 4) or are 'in care' (as described in chapter 8). These youngsters usually live in foster homes or residential establishments such as children's homes. Some children and young people live away from home in boarding schools, generally paid for by their parents. Others live in hospitals and nursing homes, in order to receive specialist medical and other forms of care. Yet others are in forms of secure accommodation, such as remand centres. The boundaries between these different locations are not always as clear-cut as might be imagined – local authorities accommodate some youngsters who have committed criminal offences, and some young people in care live in boarding schools and specialist therapeutic communities.

In this chapter we will examine some of the various settings in which children and young people live away from home. We will consider the regulations which govern the care and facilities with which they must be provided, arrangements for safeguarding their welfare, and local authority powers and duties towards them. As in other areas of law, some of the differences between the various settings in which children and young people live are complex and technical, as are the regulations that govern them. Here we will be able to offer only a general overview.

CHILDREN LOOKED AFTER BY LOCAL AUTHORITIES

The term 'looked after' refers to a situation where a local authority undertakes to provide (by itself, or by way of purchasing or arranging services) children and young people with somewhere to live away from their families, and takes on their upbringing. It covers two categories of children and young people:

- those who are accommodated by the local authority, as a service to the child and the family (as described in chapter 4);
- those who have been placed in local authority care, by way of a Care Order (as described in chapter 8).

In many circumstances, the legislation and regulations which govern these two different groups are common. For example, local authorities are under a general duty towards the children they are looking after to safeguard and promote their welfare and to make use of the same kinds of services that they make available for children cared for by their own parents. They are expected to work in close partnership with parents and others, to find out about their wishes and feelings and to do their best to meet them. However, the significant difference between the two groups should not be forgotten. With accommodated children, their parents retain full parental responsibility and can take the children back home virtually at will. The local authority has no parental responsibility for accommodated children, whereas it does for children in care.

Arranging suitable accommodation

We have already examined placements in chapter 8, and these principles apply to all children who are 'looked after'. Here we will look at implications for practice.

Meeting cultural, religious and language needs
The religious persuasion, racial origin and cultural and linguistic background of children and young people are seen as important

factors in arranging accommodation. Guidance states that 'other things being equal and in a great majority of cases, placement with a family of similar ethnic origin and religion is most likely to meet a child's needs as fully as possible and safeguard his or her welfare most effectively' [Vol 3, para 2.40].

Thus local authorities need to ensure, when recruiting, that foster-parents and staff for residential establishments will be in a position to reasonably meet the needs of the children living in the locality. While this obviously cannot involve having foster-parents from every conceivable ethnic group to hand, in order to meet every eventuality, it does mean making adequate arrangements to meet likely needs. In areas, for example, where there are large numbers of families who are African-Caribbean, this will involve recruiting sufficient numbers of African-Caribbean foster-parents.

Meeting the needs of disabled children and young people
When placing disabled children and young people, local authorities are obliged, as far as it is reasonably practicable, to make sure that the accommodation provided is 'not unsuitable' for their particular needs [s23(8)]. Important here too is the general principle that local authorities must make available the same sorts of services to those they are 'looking after' as for children in need living with their families (discussed in more detail in chapter 4) – given these are required to help children and young people overcome their disabilities and live as normal a life as possible

Maintaining links with family and community
Local authorities are generally required to promote contact between children and young people and their parents, relatives, friends and other people who are important to them. The concern here is that if the links between the child and family/community are broken, not only is this damaging to the child in the short-term, but they are hard to repair. Placements should therefore be as near as possible to the child's home, where links with the child's community can be fostered and where continuity can be maintained in terms of things like education and the child's interests and leisure pursuits.

Brothers and sisters should generally be accommodated together, although this is not a hard-and-fast rule, as each child's needs must be considered on its own merits. Nonetheless, brothers and sisters should no longer be separated to meet administrative convenience.

Offering choice

As we saw in chapter 8, a range of choices need to be available if consultation with the child and family is to be at all meaningful. This means that local authorities should not take policy decisions which effectively prevent young people having, for example, the option of living in a hostel rather than with a foster family. It also means that liaison and co-operation between agencies (including the voluntary and private sectors) is vital, so that, for example, there are opportunities for alternatives such as boarding schools and therapeutic communities. There are, of course, financial pressures which may mitigate against certain forms of placements. Currently, many specialist establishments (such as therapeutic communities) are closing down, as local authorities can no longer afford the fees.

Independent visitors

Not all children and young people who live in residential establishments have somebody to visit them and take an interest in their lives. Not only can this leave the child feeling isolated and uncared for, it can leave children vulnerable if, for example, there are problems in the foster or children's home where they are living. Whereas children who have regular contact with family and friends away from the home should be able to turn to one of them and ask for advice and help (e.g. to make a complaint), this 'safety net' may be lacking for a child who does not have these kinds of outside contacts.

The Act therefore specifies that, where a child has not been visited for twelve months, the local authority should usually appoint an independent visitor. The choice of who will take on this role will need to take into account the child's wishes and feelings. These may also include whether the independent visitor shares the child's religion, culture, language and racial background. Where it has not proved possible to make a placement which entirely reflects the child's race and culture, the independent visitor can be a crucial link with the child's racial and cultural background [Guidance, Vol 3, para 7.15].

Independent visitors are expected to contribute to the welfare of the children whom they are visiting, including promoting the child's developmental, social, emotional, educational, religious and cultural needs. It may involve encouraging children to exercise their rights and to participate in decisions which will affect them [Guidance, Vol 3, para 7.34].

Reviews

When a child is looked after by a 'responsible authority' (i.e. a local authority, voluntary organisation or proprietor of a registered children's home) his or her case must be reviewed within four weeks of arrival. A second review must be carried out no more than three months after the first, and subsequent reviews must take place not more than six months after the previous review. Before holding the review meeting, the responsible authority must generally seek and take into account the views of the child concerned, the child's parents and any others with parental responsibility, and any other person whose views the authority considers to be relevant. These people are usually expected to be able to attend the review meeting and to be notified of the details of any decisions made.

Complaints procedures

Generally, any concerns about a child or young person should first be raised informally. Problems will often be able to be resolved without any need for formal procedures. However, when this fails, the first route of action will be to make a formal complaint. The Children Act obliges all local authorities to set up, operate and publicise appropriate and effective complaints procedures, with respect to the services they provide. (As described in chapter 4, this applies to all services, not just the provision of accommodation). Voluntary organisations and registered children's homes are also required to set up complaints procedures [s59(4) and Sched 6, para 10(2)(l)].

The people entitled to make complaints about services are those children who are recipients of services, their parents and others with parental responsibility for them, local authority foster-parents and any other person that the authority considers has a sufficient interest in their welfare. Foster-parents can also complain in relation to a decision regarding an exemption from the 'usual fostering limit' [Sched 7, para 6].

The *Representations Procedure (Children) Regulations* lay out the procedure to be followed. Local authorities must take reasonable steps to ensure that all those involved in the handling of the representations, including independent persons, are familiar with the procedures set out in these Regulations. Each local authority is required to appoint an officer 'to assist the authority in the co-ordination of all aspects of their consideration of the representations'.

On receipt of a complaint the local authority must send the complainant an explanation of the procedure, and offer assistance and guidance on using it or give advice as to where such assistance and guidance might be obtained. Where the complaint is made orally, the authority must record it in writing and send the record to the complainant who must be given the opportunity to agree that it is an accurate record.

Where a complaint is made by a person claiming to have a 'sufficient interest in the child's welfare', if the authority agrees that the person has a sufficient interest, the complaint must be dealt with. If the authority does not agree, it must notify the person in writing and inform him or her that no further action will be taken. It must also notify the child concerned of its decision, if this is appropriate having regard to the child's understanding.

BOX 9.1   COMPLAINTS PROCEDURE

First stage

Once a complaint has been received, the local authority must appoint an independent person to take part in the consideration of the complaint and formulate a response within 28 days. The independent person must participate in any discussions about any action to be taken in relation to the child, in the light of the complaint.

Within this 28-day period, the authority must notify the following about a proposed result of its consideration of the complaint and the complainant's right to have the matter referred to a panel:

- the complainant;
- the person on whose behalf the complaint was made, unless the local authority considers that he or she is not of sufficient understanding or it would be likely to cause serious harm to his or her 'health or emotional condition';
- the independent person;
- any other person whom the local authority considers has sufficient interest in the case.

Second stage

If the complainant informs the authority in writing within 28 days that he or she is dissatisfied with the proposed result, the matter is to be referred to a panel. The local authority must appoint one for this purpose. This panel of three persons must include at least one independent person and must meet within 28 days of receipt of the request that the matter be referred. The panel must consider:

- any oral or written submissions that the complainant or local authority wishes to make; *and*
- any oral or written submission the independent person appointed in the first stage of the procedure wishes to make, if a different person has been appointed for the second stage.

The complainant may be accompanied by another person of his or her choice and may nominate that person to speak on his or her behalf.

The panel must decide on their recommendations and record their reasons in writing within 24 hours of the end of their meeting. The panel must notify the following of their recommendations:

- the local authority who must, together with the independent person on the panel, consider what action if any should now be taken in relation to the child concerned;
- the complainant;
- the first independent person appointed (if not on the panel);
- any other person whom the local authority considers has a sufficient interest in the case.

It is the local authority who will decide what course of action, if any, is appropriate in all the circumstances. If there are grounds for believing that the complaints procedure did not operate in accordance with the Regulations, then an application for judicial review can be made.

The Regulations spell out the legal obligations of local authorities. Guidance provides a clearer 'good practice' approach, emphasising the continuing need to work with parents and children.

Other remedies

Where somebody is dissatisfied with the outcome of making a complaint via the formal complaints procedure, a number of other remedies remain.

Judicial review
Recourse can be made over some decisions to judicial review (described in chapter 2).

Local authority ombudsman
A complaint can be made to the local authority ombudsman. This is essentially a political move, to try to put pressure on the local authority. There is no direct consequence for the complainant, although in some cases, where there has been a clear finding of maladminstration, the ombudsman has made a recommendation of compensation for the aggrieved parties. The ombudsman will also submit a report on the complaint, which may contain recommendations for action to be taken by the local authority to remedy any defects in their procedures, although the local authority is not bound by this decision.

Political lobbying

Pressure can be applied via local councillors, since they have an overseeing role for social services. The person to contact would be the complainant's local councillor or the Chair of the Social Services Committee. Where concerns are about services for a particular group of children, representations are more likely to be effective if a number of people press the case collectively, by, for example, setting up a pressure group.

The Children Act provides for intervention by the Secretary of State, in exceptional circumstances. The usual route to this would be via the complainant's MP. Such an application would be very unlikely to succeed, but its making would raise the issue at a government level, which can bring about action.

The European Court of Human Rights

When all domestic remedies have been exhausted and still a grievance has not been either acknowledged or properly responded to, a judgement may be sought in relation to the European Convention on Human Rights. There have, in fact, been a number of successful applications to the Commission by parents and children from the UK over the past decade. The particular case would have to come within one of the articles or protocols of the Convention and it is a lengthy process which can take a number of years.

Leaving care and aftercare

Although a number of local authorities had established, prior to the Children Act, a range of services to help prepare young people for the time at which they left care and to support them once they had left and set up home independently, these were by no means universal. One of the strongest criticisms of the care system had been that, all too often, it did not do enough for those young people for whom it had acted in the role of 'parent'. The Children Act seeks to improve this situation, by placing a range of duties on local authorities to provide aftercare and giving them powers to support young people in the period immediately after they leave care. These provisions apply to young people at least up until they reach the age of 21, and may extend beyond that.

Guidance states:

> *The successful re-integration of a young person with his family ... or the establishment of the ability in the young person to become as self-supporting as possible ... is the culmination of a young person's experience in being cared for. ... It is of vital importance that young people are properly prepared for this step and given access to support afterwards.* [Vol 3, paras 9.3–9.4]

Local authorities are under a *duty* to advise, assist and befriend young people when they cease to be looked after by them [s24(1)]. This obligation applies to all those under twenty-one who, at any time after they reached sixteen but while still a child (i.e. under eighteen), were looked after by a local authority, or who were accommodated by or on behalf of a voluntary organisation for three months or more [s24(2)(a)&(b)].

Local authorities also have *powers* to offer similar support to young people who have been accommodated in a registered children's home, by a health or education authority, a residential care home, nursing home or mental nursing home, or were privately fostered [s24(2)(c)–(e)&(4)].

Assistance may be in the form of providing goods (such as furniture) or other assistance 'in kind', and it can consist of paying cash [s24(7)]. It can, for instance, include contributing to expenses to allow the young person to live close to where they are seeking employment or receiving education or training. Local authorities can make grants to help young people with expenses connected with their education or training [s24(8)].

⚬ GARETH'S STORY –

Gareth came into care at the age of fourteen, following a series of violent assaults by his step-father. He was placed in foster care, but this broke down after eight months and he went to live in a hostel.

Two years later, at the age of sixteen, Gareth had a series of disputes with staff in the hostel and he left to go and live in a squat with friends. He became very depressed and went back to live at home. This soon ended in another row after he had been caught shop-lifting, and his step-father threw him out.

Gareth's probation officer helped him to find a bed-sit and a place on a training scheme. However, she left the post soon after and Gareth did not get on with the man who replaced her. Despite this, Gareth did manage to get a low-paid job, which lasted for three months.

Three weeks ago Gareth was laid off. He is now behind with his rent and other bills and has not managed to get income support – he walked out of the benefits office because he felt they were being very rude and uncaring. He didn't know where to turn. The next day he arrived at the social services office and asked to see someone. He said to the duty social worker that, unless they could help him, he knew he would be out on the streets by next week. He was very upset and demoralised.

Under section 24, the authority has a duty to advise, assist and befriend Gareth. This duty extends to giving assistance not only in kind but in cash [s24(7)]. As they had looked after Gareth, the local authority also has the power to give assistance by contributing to expenses incurred by Gareth in living near the place where he is employed or seeking employment, or where he is receiving education or training [s24(8)]. If Gareth is lucky, he will be given these forms of assistance. If he is very lucky, he will live in an area where an aftercare scheme is in operation, designed to help young people in just these kinds of circumstances. However, he may well not be 'lucky' – only about 50% of local authorities are currently meeting their obligations to the young people for whom they are responsible. It is in this area of work, possibly more than anywhere else, that resource constraints have severely limited the ability of local authorities to fulfil their statutory duties.

If Gareth does not receive the assistance he needs to get himself sorted out, he has three options. First he can make a complaint under section 26 that the authority has failed to provide the assistance that it is under a statutory duty to provide. Secondly, if he discovers that there are no arrangements for such assistance within the area of the authority concerned, he could seek judicial review or, finally, the Secretary of State's default powers under section 84. Of course, these are something of a 'Catch 22' set of options in that, although he is entitled to take these courses of action, he is hardly in a position to do so – if he had the kinds of contacts, skills and knowledge entailed in such courses of action, he would be unlikely to be in this situation. Gareth's best choice will probably be to seek help from an organisation such as the Children's Legal Centre or the National Association for Young People in Care, from a Law Centre (if one is available) or from a Citizen's Advice Bureau.

Secure accommodation

It is important to distinguish between two quite different forms of secure accommodation: that which may be provided for children who are being looked after, and that which constitutes a form of criminal detention, following conviction of the child or young person for an offence. We will look at provisions for such young offenders in the next section.

Prior to the Criminal Justice Act 1982, decisions about whether to lock up 'problem children' who were in care were left entirely in the hands of the local authority concerned. However, since 1983 local authorities have had to apply to court for approval if they want to lock up a child for more than 72 hours. Under the Children Act, the situation has been further clarified and tightened. Now there are very clear criteria which must be satisfied before it is legal to lock up a child for any period at all (see Box 9.2).

BOX 9.2	LIMITS ON PLACING ACCOMMODATED YOUNG PEOPLE IN SECURE ACCOMMODATION

Placement in secure accommodation will seldom be appropriate for a young child. No child under the age of thirteen years can be placed in secure accommodation without the prior approval of the Secretary of State. A young person may not be placed or kept in secure accommodation unless it appears that:

1 he or she has a history of absconding, is likely to abscond from any other description of accommodation, and is likely to suffer significant harm if he or she absconds; *or*

2 he or she is likely to injure him or herself or other persons if kept in any other description of accommodation.

These provisions apply not only to young people who are accommodated by local authorities, but also to those accommodated by health authorities (including a National Health Service Trust), local education authorities and in other forms of residential care, nursing or mental homes.

While it is acknowledged that there will inevitably be occasions where placing a young person in secure accommodation will be necessary for that youngster's safety or for the safety of others, secure accommodation is essentially a *protective* measure. Restricting young people's liberty is a serious step, which must be taken only when there is no appropriate alternative. It must be a last resort, in the sense that all other possibilities must first have been comprehensively considered and rejected. It must never be done because no other placement is available, because of inadequacies in staffing or because the child is simply being a nuisance or runs away. It must also never be used as a form of punishment [Regulations, Vol 4, para 8.5].

Recently, the Department of Health issued new Guidance concerning the management of children and young people who are causing problems for those looking after them – for example, when a youngster is being disobedient and staying out all night or makes to run away after an argument. These kinds of situations obviously pose considerable problems for care staff. Difficult judgements need to be made about whether or not the circumstances warrant using physical control (such as standing in a door to prevent the young person from leaving or holding a child who is having a temper tantrum). Staff working in such situations need to make sure they are familiar with the *Guidance on Permissible Forms of Control* (see page 240).

YOUNG OFFENDERS

In this section we will examine the legislation governing young people who live away from home as a result of remands or convictions for criminal offences. The Children Act 1989 abolished the rarely used care order in criminal proceedings and removed from the Juvenile Court its care jurisdiction (as we have seen in chapters 2 and 8, this was transferred to the Magistrates' Family Proceedings Court), so that the Juvenile Court became a criminal court. The Criminal Justice Act 1991 renames the court the *Youth Court*, which now includes seventeen-year-olds within its jurisdiction for the first time. Though it is now exclusively a criminal court, it still has a duty to consider the welfare of the children and young people with whom it deals. Young offenders can still be placed in local authority accommodation, either on remand or as a result of the court making a Supervision Order with a residence requirement.

Secure accommodation provided by a local authority

The regulations for secure accommodation for young offenders apply to young people who have been:

1 detained by the police under section 38(6) of the Police and Criminal Evidence Act 1984; *or*
2 remanded to local authority accommodation under section 23 of the Children and Young Persons Act 1969:
    (a) having been charged or convicted of an offence of violence (or having been previously convicted of such an offence), *or*
    (b) having been charged with or convicted of an offence which would be imprisonable for fourteen years or more if they were aged twenty-one or over.

The criteria which apply to young people who are 'looked after' (see above) are modified by the Children (Secure Accommodation) Regulations 1991. This allows young offenders to be placed in local authority secure accommodation if it appears that other accommodation would be inappropriate because:

1 they are likely to abscond from other accommodation; *or*
2 they are likely to injure themselves or other people if kept in other accommodation.

They cannot be kept in secure accommodation beyond the period of the remand and, in any event, no longer than 28 days without further court authorisation.

Remands to local authority accommodation

As a result of further changes to the Children and Young Persons Act 1969 (introduced by section 60 of the Criminal Justice Act 1991), the youth court will be able to remand fifteen- and sixteen-year-olds with a 'security requirement'. This provides new arrangements for 'secure remands' for fifteen- and sixteen-year-olds and gives the courts powers to attach conditions when juveniles are remanded in local authority accommodation. These provisions have been initially implemented in a modified form.

As of 1st October 1992, transitional provisions abolish the 'unruliness' certification procedure [s62(3)]. The court can remand a boy aged fifteen or sixteen to a remand centre or prison only if he is legally represented (or has been offered legal representation but has refused or failed to apply for it) and, after consultation with the local authority or probation service, the court states that:

1 he is charged with, or convicted of, a violent or sexual offence or an offence punishable, in the case of an adult, with imprisonment for fourteen years or more; *or*
2 he has a recent history of absconding while remanded to local authority accommodation and is charged with, or has been convicted of, an imprisonable offence alleged or found to have been committed while he was so remanded; *and*
the court is of the opinion that only remanding him to a remand centre or prison would be adequate to protect the public from serious harm from him.

In this context, 'serious harm' is not limited to violent or sexual offences. However, where the alleged offence is a violent or sexual one, the requirement to protect the public from serious harm is a reference to 'death or serious personal injury, whether physical or psychological, occasioned by further offences committed by [the juvenile]'.

While these transitional provisions apply, local authorities are under a duty to provide sufficient local authority accommodation and secure accommodation so that remands in custody can be phased out.

When *fully* implemented, section 60 of the Criminal Justice Act 1991 will amend entirely section 23 of the Children and Young Persons Act 1969, thereby creating a new power for courts to remand fifteen- or sixteen-year-olds (but not younger juveniles) of either sex with a security requirement (i.e. a requirement that they be held in local authority secure accommodation) if certain conditions are met [s60(1)]. These are:

1 *either* the young person is charged with or has been convicted of a violent or sexual offence or an offence carrying a maximum penalty of at least fourteen years imprisonment for an adult; *or*
2 the young person has a recent history of absconding while remanded to local authority accommodation and is charged with, or convicted of, an imprisonable offence committed (or alleged to have been) while so remanded; *and*
3 in either case, only a remand with a security requirement would be adequate to protect the public from serious harm from him or her.

Section 60 gives the courts new powers to attach conditions when juveniles of any age are remanded in local authority accommodation without a security requirement. They will have two main new powers:

1 to require the remanded person to comply with conditions of the kind that could be imposed under the Bail Act 1976; *and*
2 to require the local authority not to place the remanded juvenile with a named person.

Before imposing a security requirement or remanding fifteen- and sixteen-year-old boys in prison, the court will be required to consult the local authority.

Detention by the police

Section 59 of the Criminal Justice Act has amended section 38(6) of the Police and Criminal Evidence Act 1984 (which deals with the arrangements for the detention of juveniles under the age of seventeen who have been arrested by the police). Section 59 allows the police to hold fifteen- and sixteen-year-olds, *but not younger juveniles*, where no local authority secure accommodation is available and where keeping the juveniles in any other local authority accommodation would not be adequate to protect the public from serious harm from them.

It also continues to allow the police to hold juveniles of any age where it would be impracticable to make a transfer under section 38 of the Police and Criminal Evidence Act 1984 – the nature of the local authority accommodation in which the juvenile is to be held cannot be a factor in deciding whether the transfer is 'impracticable'. The police custody officer has to certify the reason for not making the transfer and, in the case of 'impracticability', the certificate will have to specify the circumstances which make the transfer impracticable.

Young people accommodated under Supervision Orders

Supervision Orders can now be imposed on offenders aged seventeen, because of the extension of the jurisdiction of the Youth Court.

Criminal Supervision Orders with a residence requirement

The power of the court to attach a 'residence requirement' to a Supervision Order was introduced by the Children Act 1989 which inserted a new section (12AA) into the Children and Young Persons Act 1969 [Sched 12, para 23 of the Children Act

1989]. Such a requirement is not intended to be punitive, but rather to assist a young person to work through his or her problems. It does this by removing him or her from the surroundings that are contributing to the offending behaviour and placing him or her in local authority accommodation.

The court has a discretion as to how long such a requirement is to last, but it cannot last more than six months. The court also has the power to specify that the juvenile is not to live with a named person or persons, but it cannot specify where the juvenile is to reside. The court must consult with the local authority before imposing such a requirement. The following conditions must be met before a court can impose a residence requirement:

1   a Criminal Supervision Order has previously been made in respect of the juvenile;
2   that order imposed *either*:
   (a)   a requirement under section 12A(3) of the Children and Young People Act 1969 (e.g. to take part in a programme of intermediate treatment); *or*
   (b)   a residence requirement;
3   the juvenile is convicted of an offence which:
   (a)   was committed while that order was in force;
   (b)   would have been punishable with imprisonment if it had been committed by a person over the age of twenty-one, *and*
   (c)   in the opinion of the court is serious;
4   the court is satisfied that the behaviour that constituted the offence was due, to a significant extent, to the circumstances in which the juvenile was living. (This does not apply if condition 2(b) is met).

However, unless condition 2(b) applies, the court must obtain a pre-sentence report to satisfy itself that the conditions have been met, or already have a social enquiry report containing sufficient information. The report must deal with the circumstances in which the juvenile was living. The Guidance [Vol 1, para 6.26] states that:

> It will not be enough to make a general comment on the family or other circumstances. Any cause and effect between

the juvenile's circumstances and his offending must be based on clear demonstrable evidence ... one of the primary objectives of a residence requirement is to provide an opportunity for both the juvenile and his family or other carers to address the specific difficulties which give rise to his offending. Any assessment, therefore, which concludes that there is a significant link between the juvenile's current living circumstances and his offences should be accompanied by a clear action plan about the work to be done to resolve the difficulties.

A further condition that must be satisfied before a Youth Court can impose a residence requirement is that young people must be legally represented unless they have failed to obtain a lawyer (where their resources are such that they are not in need of assistance) or they have refused to apply for legal aid. It is important that the young person is made aware of the implications of refusing to be represented. The obligation on local authorities to conduct a regular review of the case of each child they are looking after extends to children under a residence requirement.

CHILDREN AND YOUNG PEOPLE LIVING AWAY FROM HOME IN BOARDING SCHOOLS

The Children Act acknowledges that there is a wide range of different kinds of boarding school providing education and accommodation for pupils, and a variety of reasons why children are there.

Residential schools

This term is generally used to designate an establishment where children are placed to meet particular needs they may have, such as when they are disabled and need certain kinds of care, or when they are suffering from emotional or behaviour problems with which their parents cannot cope. A proportion of children will be placed in such establishments because they are seen as a danger to themselves or to others.

Thus residential schools offer a range of resources for the care and development of certain children. Residential school placements, however, are expected to always be made with the clear intention of primarily meeting the pupil's *educational* needs, and only after careful joint assessment by the LEA, social services and the relevant health authority (as directed within the 1981 Education Act). LEAs are required to collaborate closely with social services to ensure that there is coherent and clear planning for arrangements during school holidays, maintaining links between the child and his or her family and community, and future arrangements for the child when he or she leaves school.

Independent schools

An independent school is defined as any school at which full-time education is provided for five or more pupils of compulsory school age, which is *not* a school maintained by an LEA, grant maintained or a non-maintained special school. Independent schools with more than 50 boarding pupils and/or approved by LEAs for the placement of pupils with statements of special educational needs [s11(3)(a) of the Education Act 1981], which provide or arrange accommodation for such pupils, are covered by section 87 of the Children Act.

Independent schools with residential accommodation not falling within the above category are governed by the provisions relating to registered children's homes [Part VIII]. The requirements relating to private fostering [Part IX] may also be relevant in a minority of cases. (The private fostering arrangements are only relevant in relation to short-term holiday arrangements, establishments providing education for fewer than five children which by definition cannot be independent schools, and schools operating core and cluster arrangements.)

Duties of proprietors
Proprietors of and persons running independent schools are under a duty to safeguard and promote the children's welfare [s87(1)]. Social services are under a duty to take steps to determine whether the children's welfare is adequately

safeguarded and promoted while they are accommodated by these schools [s87(3)]. To do so they have specific powers [s87(5)&(8) and the Inspection of Premises, Children and Records (Independent Schools) Regulations 1991]. They may:

- enter and inspect schools, including looking at pupils' bedrooms, kitchens, toilets, sick-bays and areas used for sporting and recreation facilities and classrooms;
- visually examine the pupils attending the school. Guidance stresses that this power should not be used as a substitute for Education Supervision Orders and Child Assessment Orders;
- inspect records containing information about the state of health, emotional or developmental wellbeing or welfare of pupils. These include records of medical or dental treatment, accidents, deaths, serious illness or infectious disease of pupils, or other significant harm sustained by a pupil while at the school;
- inspect records of the names and qualifications of the staff responsible for the welfare of pupils, including non-teaching and part-time staff and volunteers working at the school, both inside and outside teaching hours;
- inspect records of any absconding from the school, fire practice drills and fire alarm tests;
- inspect details of any complaints made concerning the state of health, emotional and developmental wellbeing of pupils and details of punishments administered to pupils.

Standards to be maintained
Independent schools are expected to keep records of the welfare and development of the children with sufficient clarity and detail to inform decision-making. They should have clearly laid down and recognised procedures for dealing with allegations of abuse. Thorough checks on the suitability of all staff (and anyone providing accommodation for pupils) should be carried out prior to appointment. All pupils should be registered with a school medical officer or a local general practitioner, and be able to consult a doctor in whom they have confidence (e.g. one of the same sex).

The quality of the living space and overall environment should be suitable, with proper heating and sanitation, separate bedrooms for boys and girls and older and younger children, and proper common rooms. There should be facilities to ensure that children can maintain contact with parents, relatives and friends in privacy.

Schools should ensure that parents know their policy on behaviour and discipline and should aim to secure parents' support for putting it into practice. This information should be made available to social services. Legislation has not abolished the use of corporal punishment in all categories of independent schools, but social services and proprietors are instructed to consider carefully the implications of the existing legislation, section 47 of the Education Act (No 2) 1986 and Regulation 3 of the Education (Abolition of Corporal Punishment) (Independent Schools) (Prescribed Categories of Persons) Regulations 1989, which together prohibit the use of corporal punishment on all pupils whose fees at an independent school are paid by a local authority. Corporal punishment is widely regarded as being particularly inappropriate for children with special educational needs.

Complaints

Schools are obliged to operate a clear and simple procedure to enable pupils to raise issues that cannot be dealt with informally. Information about such a complaints procedure should be put in writing and given to all children and staff as well as those with parental responsibility for the children. A suitable senior member of staff should be responsible for complaints, which should be dealt with quickly and confidentially, in accordance with procedures laid down by the local Area Child Protection Committee. It is important that provision is made for contact with an adult outside the school, including help-lines, for situations requiring confidentiality or independence.

In cases where allegations are made against a member of staff, the staff member should be suspended, without implying any presumption of guilt, while the allegation is investigated. Investigation of formal complaints of all kinds should involve someone independent of the school (e.g. an officer or member of the LEA or social services).

Schools are expected to be sensitive to the religious, cultural, racial and linguistic background and beliefs of their pupils, as should social services departments in the way in which they carry out their inspections. Schools should provide a statement of these matters in their prospectuses. There should be equal opportunity for boys and girls.

Notifying the Secretary of State
Where social services are of the opinion that a child's welfare is not being safeguarded and promoted as required by section 87(1), it must notify the Secretary of State for Education [s87(4)]. However, the Guidance advises that, before doing so, social services should first discuss its concerns with the school and alert the Department for Education or the Welsh Office. Unless the matter is urgent, social services should seek to resolve any problem informally before taking formal action. The Secretary of State for Health (generally through the Social Services Inspectorate) has the power to inspect independent schools, require proprietors to furnish information or to allow records to be inspected.

Once the Secretary of State for Education has been notified, if satisfied that there has been a failure to comply with the duty imposed by section 87 of the Children Act, he or she can exercise powers under sections 70–75 of the Education Act 1944 (as amended by the Children Act 1989). These include issuing a notice of complaint against the school, and specifying the reasons for the complaint and what the school must do to remedy the situation. At least six months must be allowed for the school to comply, or the proprietor can appeal to the Independent Schools Tribunal. If the matters complained about are not put right, the Secretary of State may make orders, including ones which result in the school being struck off the Register of Independent Schools or the disqualification of the proprietor or a teacher.

Non-maintained special schools

Whilst non-maintained special schools are not 'independent schools' and are not thereby covered by section 87 of the

Children Act, they are subject to the same duties as voluntary organisations to safeguard and promote children's welfare [s61]. Local authorities have duties towards such schools [s62] and they may be inspected by local authorities [s80]. Such schools are approved by the Secretary of State for Education and Science under section 9(5) of the Education Act 1944 and are subject to the Education (Approval of Special Schools) Regulations 1983 and the Education (Approval of Special Schools) (Amendment) Regulations 1991. They are also subject to the Arrangements for Placement of Children (General) Regulations 1991, the Review of Children's Cases Regulations 1991 and the Representations Procedure (Children) Regulations 1991 and associated Guidance.

Independent schools registered as children's homes

Some independent boarding schools are required to register under the Registered Homes Act 1984 – if they are not approved under the Education Act 1981 and have 50 or fewer boarders who need personal care by virtue of physical or mental disability. Other independent schools are required to register as registered children's homes under the Children Act 1989, section 63. The Education Act has amended section 63 of the Children Act 1989 so that an independent school is a children's home if it provides accommodation for more than three children for more than 295 days in any year over a two year period, unless approved by the Secretary of State under section 189 of the Education Act 1993.

The person running such a home is under the following duties:

- 'to safeguard and promote the child's welfare';
- to make appropriate use of the services and facilities available for children cared for by their own parents;
- to advise, assist and befriend pupils with a view to promoting their welfare when they cease to be so accommodated [s64(1)];
- before making any decision with respect to pupils, to ascertain their wishes and feelings and those of their parents, others with parental responsibility and other relevant people

[s64(2)], taking account of pupils' religious persuasions, racial origins and cultural and linguistic backgrounds [s64(3)].

Local authorities must satisfy themselves that any person running a children's home is satisfactorily safeguarding and promoting the welfare of the pupils living there, and must arrange for these pupils to be visited [s64(4) applying s62(1)]. Local authorities have powers to enter and inspect premises, and to examine pupils and records. Where a local authority is not satisfied, it must take steps to remove the child concerned to live with a parent or relative or a person with parental responsibility, unless this would not be in the best interests of the child. The local authority must consider the extent to which it should exercise any of its functions with respect to the child [s64(4), applying s62(5)].

People disqualified from fostering a child privately must not run, be employed by, be concerned in the management of, or have any financial interest in a children's home, unless they have the written consent of the local authority [s65(1)]. Nor can anybody running a children's home employ a person who is so disqualified.

CHILDREN AND YOUNG PEOPLE LIVING AWAY FROM HOME IN HOSPITALS AND NURSING HOMES

In general, children and young people living in hospitals, nursing homes and other similar establishments are covered under other headings. Where children and young people are accommodated for more than three consecutive months by health authorities and NHS Trusts, their welfare and care is covered by the legislation and regulations which apply to children's homes provided by social services departments. The two agencies are required to liaise with, inform and consult each other. Similarly, children and young people living in privately run establishments, or those run by voluntary agencies, are regulated in the same way as boarding schools. The local authority may enter any residential care home, nursing home or mental nursing home to see that the children's welfare is being adequately safeguarded. The local authority does not have a similar power to enter local health and education authority establishments to check on the child's welfare.

As the children and young people concerned are generally looked after in such establishments because they are disabled, they fall within the category of being 'in need'. It is worth being reminded, therefore, of the local authority's obligation to provide them with services and, in particular, to promote their upbringing within their own families. Of course, there will be circumstances where a residential nursing home, for example, is the best option for a child and the family. Nonetheless, the general principle is that a child should not be so accommodated if, given appropriate services, the family is willing and able to look after him or her at home.

– STELLA'S STORY –

Stella was born with severe birth damage. She has cerebral palsy, profound learning disabilities, and is blind and deaf. She is now fourteen, and has lived in a long-stay hospital for six years.

Her family visit her often and, recently, have begun to feel that they would like to be able to have her to stay at home, at least some of the time. Up until now they have found visits very difficult to manage.

Under the Children Act 1989, Stella and her family are entitled to services which foster her contact with her family and which could enable her to live at home. If the family agree that this is what they want, their local authority is under a duty to assess her needs and to offer appropriate services.

As we have seen throughout this book, the law provides extensively for enabling children and their families to receive services to improve the quality of children's lives. At the same time, local authorities are limited by the constraints on their resources as to what they can, in practice, offer towards achieving this aim. Whether or not Stella will be able to spend more time with her family will depend not on the law itself, but on the capability of the local authority to meet their obligations and the determination and stamina of her parents in getting them to do so.

10 *Is the law good for children?*

This final chapter brings together some of the issues covered in earlier chapters in a rather different context. Here we are not so much concerned with the rules and processes of law and the 'good practice' it is intended to ensure, as with the extent to which the law is a 'good thing' – can the law be a positive force in promoting children's welfare and rights?

CHILDREN'S WELFARE AND CHILDREN'S RIGHTS

Often it is assumed that these mean much the same thing – that anything done to improve the welfare of children is, by definition, going to promote their rights. This notion can, however, be contested. Action taken to protect children will often, inevitably, undermine their autonomy; offering children a degree of self-determination can put them at risk. Yet both can be recouched in terms of rights – indeed, as we will see later, this is precisely what has been done within the United Nations Convention on the Rights of the Child, which sets out that children are both entitled to be protected from harm and entitled to be treated as autonomous citizens, whose views deserve to be discovered and listened to and who should be enabled to participate in decisions made about their own lives and upbringing. Simply because rights may be in conflict with each other does not mean that they cannot both be asserted, though this will imply a need to establish ways of resolving what to do when they are at odds. So, the question is, what does current law do to promote children's welfare and rights?

Consideration of the child's welfare

Historically, the idea that the law should take account of the welfare of the child is relatively new. In the past it was either irrelevant (until the 19th century, common law in England gave exclusive rights over children to the father) or it was used as little more than a slogan in search of a definition – a slogan under which adulterous mothers could lose custody of their children. Now things do appear to be different – child law does assume that children have a *right* to have their welfare treated as the paramount consideration in decisions made about their upbringing. As the Lord Chancellor stressed, when the Children Bill was receiving its second reading, 'the days when a child could be treated as a possession of a parent – indeed, when they had in the past a right to his services and to sue on their loss – are now buried forever' (Hansard, House of Lords, 6th December, 1988).

The paramountcy principle

The Children Act 1989 does more than simply state (as earlier legislation had done) that the welfare of the child is the court's paramount consideration in any question relating to the upbringing of a child. It also provides, for the first time, a welfare checklist of factors that the court must consider in certain proceedings. This list, in itself, is not totally new – much of it has its origins in pre-1989 case law. However, by requiring the court to consider the items on the checklist, current legislation does impose a clear framework on the otherwise untrammelled discretion of the court.

In particular, it enshrines for the first time the right of children to have a voice – their wishes and feelings about the decision before the court must be ascertained and taken into account. Indeed, it was argued by the Lord Chancellor during the passage of the Bill that while '[t]he Bill does not make the child's wishes absolutely determinative of the matter; it puts the child's wishes at the forefront of the circumstances to which the court will have regard. That is a valuable position for those wishes.' (Hansard, House of Lords, 19th December, 1988).

Criminal proceedings

The paramountcy principle does not apply to all legal proceedings. Specifically, in criminal proceedings where the child is a witness to an offence, the child's needs are no more than a factor in the context of a more fundamental concern for justice. In such cases the defendant's rights to a fair trial are held, in law, to be critical. Indeed, in the USA certain rights provided by the 6th amendment to the US constitution, particularly the right of the accused to be directly confronted by his or her accuser, present considerable problems when efforts have been made to alleviate the distress of child witnesses. Following US Supreme Court rulings, in most states a case must be made, on its own merits, to allow a child any form of relief, such as a screen obscuring the defendant or the use of closed-circuit video-links. In the UK, having no formal constitution, the problems have been different and child witnesses are allowed to testify using such devices. Nonetheless, despite the recommendations of the Pigot Report (see chapter 5), child witnesses must still be available to be cross-examined.

Thus, although some considerable steps have been taken to alleviate the distress of child witnesses in criminal proceedings, in such cases their welfare is not the court's prime consideration. We ourselves would argue that, in a free and just society, this is as it should be. While the child's needs must be taken seriously, the risks of wrongful conviction have to be balanced out against them.

We would argue that this is not, fundamentally, where the problem lies. We are much more concerned about the way in which the demands of possible criminal proceedings have, in some localities at least, come to dominate the way in which allegations of sexual assaults on children are investigated. The introduction of the Home Office *Memorandum of Good Practice* in 1992 has, for all its good intentions, frequently resulted in a situation where investigations under section 47 of the Children Act 1989 are so overshadowed by the requirement to obtain and protect evidence that the basic purpose of the investigation can get undermined.

For example, the approach taken can mitigate against working in partnership with parents, against fully informing children about the consequences of their participation, and against conducting interviews in ways best suited to enabling children to express their account of the events in question. It is certainly true that many of the principles of 'evidentially sound' interviewing are equally appropriate for ascertaining what, if anything, happened – which is as important for protecting the child as for gaining evidence. Nonetheless, there will often be conflicts between these two objectives, which are not easily resolved. In such situations there is a strong argument that a child's individual welfare must be given precedence. While we may accept that a child, of his or her own volition, may be willing to agree to undergo a distressing experience for the benefit of others, it is much more difficult to decide on a child's behalf that his or her interests must be compromised in order to protect 'society' (including other children).

Deciding what is in the child's best interests

Simply arguing that the child's welfare must be the paramount consideration does not, however, end the matter. The trouble is that there is no objective and universal definition of what constitutes 'the child's welfare'. We can see this from the public arguments over issues such as the corporal punishment of children, whether gays and lesbians are able to be good parents, and disputes over transracial adoption. Even a brief review of the cases before our courts and the judgements made by professionals, such as social workers, over the past decade reveals a wide variety of views and attitudes towards children and their welfare.

This should not surprise us – we live in a complex multi-cultural society, further divided on the basis of class and gender. It would be surprising if we all agreed on definitions of 'the child's welfare' and what it is to be a good parent. Some people insist that proper discipline, including physical punishment, is good for children, while others (such as the organisation EPOCH – End Physical Punishment of Children) lobby to make it unlawful. Some people argue that children need conventional sex-role models in the home in order to grow up into healthy and mature adults, while others argue, equally vehemently, that it is the kind of care a parent gives that matters and their sexuality is irrelevant. Some people contest that black children will be turned into 'bounty-bar kids' (black on the outside but white on the inside) unless they grow up with at least one black parent and with access to and pride in their black culture and community, while others assert that race is just one issue among others and should never be a determining factor in finding substitute parents for a child. The question is, how should such disputes be resolved? In what ways does the law offer a framework for determining what should happen?

Direction versus discretion

Legislation generally addresses contentious areas by combining specific criteria with opportunities for discretion to be applied. A good example of this is in care proceedings. In order for a court to make a Care Order, specific and fairly tightly defined criteria must be established by way of evidence. Even if, after hearing all of the evidence in a case, the court believes that taking a particular child into care would be good for him or her, it cannot make a Care Order unless the 'threshold criteria' (see chapter 8) are satisfied and it is convinced that this would be better than making no order at all. If these are established, the court has very considerable leeway about what it can do – it can make a range of orders, singly or in combination, to achieve a particular outcome. It will decide by considering the welfare checklist, which is deliberately written in very general terms to allow all sorts of different aspects of the child's circumstances to be taken into account.

The crunch, of course, is that the way this discretion is handled will depend, in fair measure, on the beliefs, preconceptions and world-views of the decision-makers – in this case the judge or the magistrates. The law is often criticised because such people are seen as not being representative of the population at large. Judges come from a predominantly white, middle-class background, are overwhelmingly male and their professional lives have been spent within the rarefied atmosphere of the legal Bar. Even though in some areas strenuous attempts have been made to recruit magistrates who are more in touch with the lives of ordinary people, they too come mainly from backgrounds significantly more privileged than those over whom they sit in judgement.

To be fair, the introduction of the Children Act was accompanied by a number of measures intended to make sure that child welfare cases would be heard by people who were at least better informed than before. Judges and magistrates have been specially selected and trained. Court officers, including Justices' Clerks, have also undergone extensive training. This training has covered not just the law itself, but also issues such as sexuality, race and cultural diversity with regard to things like child rearing. Nevertheless, it remains true that the courts, as operated in the UK, are a conservative institution, poorly equipped to address the diversity of views which operate in our society with respect to children's welfare. A great deal remains to be done in terms of both recruitment and training if all those who come before the courts are to receive equitable and unprejudiced judgement.

What are the alternatives?

If we are to judge the legal system then, in fairness, we must do so against the alternatives. These fall into two main categories. The first is to adopt a more *laissez-faire* approach. Historically, this was generally how child welfare was addressed, within a context in which the family was regarded as an essentially private institution into which the law had no right to intrude. For example, in 1874, in a debate in Parliament about the need to introduce welfare services, a noted reformer, Whatley Cooke Taylor, said 'I would rather see even a higher rate of infant mortality prevailing ... than intrude one iota further on the sanctity of the domestic hearth' (quoted in Inglis, 1978, p. 24). In this context the question is, ultimately, whether it is better to allow children to be raped, murdered and brutally assaulted, or to intervene? We have no doubt, these days, that doing nothing is simply not an option.

The question arises, how should such intervention be done and by whom? The second alternative to legal scrutiny is to set up a public body and afford it full authority to take action when a child's welfare is at stake. In other words, it is possible to operate a system outside the law which has complete discretion. Such a system operates in the Netherlands at present, called the 'confidential doctor' system. Certain medical professionals are given powers to receive complaints about child mistreatment and to discretely find solutions. Its proponents argue that it is a better system than going to law, because problems can be dealt with in partnership with parents. This means, they say, that people are far more prepared to seek help and to co-operate, in the knowledge that they will not have to face a criminal prosecution. Its critics, on the other hand, argue that the system fails to protect children and allows law-breaking adults to avoid criminal sanctions. It deprives children of the protection of the law that adults have.

In principle, and in perhaps somewhat utopian terms, what the Children Act is seeking to achieve is a workable balance between enforced legal intervention on the one hand and a system of voluntary support to families when they are facing times of trouble on the other. Its aim is to offer children the full protection of the law if they are at risk of significant harm, while offering the potential that, wherever possible, problems can be tackled more informally. Like any system it has its flaws and at times can be heavy-handed, but it is probably the best that can be achieved. We are suggesting here that the law is, in the end, a necessary place of last resort. We cannot offer anything better in its place. What we need to do is to make its operation better.

PROMOTING CHILDREN'S RIGHTS

This leads us back to a consideration of a point raised earlier – to what extent should the law be concerned with children's rights as opposed to their welfare? This is because, when there are disagreements about what is meant by 'welfare', one solution is to turn the question around in a way that asks not so much what are children's *needs* (which, inevitably, implies that somebody else has to judge), but what are children's *rights* – what, in a just and good society, are children entitled to expect? What are children justified in demanding from the law?

The notion of 'rights' is not in any way simple or consensual. While some regard rights as absolute, others view them as only existing in conjunction with responsibilities. Others still question 'rights-speak' itself, seeing it as a form of thinking which prioritises individual rights over the rights of the community to expect its members to co-operate for the common good. Whatever the definition, to talk of rights is to acknowledge that what are at issue are questions of power and control – what is at stake is who has the power to make decisions and take action, who has control over whom. Crucial are the questions of who decides what risks can be taken and who takes responsibility when something goes wrong.

The shift from 'needs' to 'rights' does, however, provide one way of answering the question as to who is entitled to decide what needs to happen to promote and safeguard a child's welfare – the child. We will therefore go on to explore the extent to which the law can and should and does afford children the right to determine their welfare for themselves.

Children's rights in practice

In practice, this means asserting that children are entitled, for example, to consult a doctor in confidence about contraception or to decide for themselves with which of their divorcing parents they would prefer to live. It involves recognising that children are persons with developing capacities who will, even while they are still legally 'children', reach a stage of being as capable as many adults to make informed choices. This is not to suggest that they will always make the best or the most informed choices, or that they will never be swayed by inducements or take a short-sighted view. Nor is it to argue that the average two-year-old has an equal capacity to make a well-informed decision as the average teenager. It does, however, argue that the vast majority of children, as they grow up, will reach a point where their ability to choose wisely is no better and no worse than the adults around them – who have their own axes to grind, their own prejudices and their own limits.

Of course, when children want to do something that is seen by the adults around them as being consistent with their welfare, then no problem arises – adults are generally perfectly happy to let them choose in such situations. Things become more problematic when a child's view of what he or she wants to do clashes with that of the adults around who are in a more powerful position – a problem that gets all the more complicated when the adults themselves cannot agree.

The Gillick case
This dilemma was the basis of the Gillick case. The clash was not so much a direct one between Victoria Gillick and her children, but between this mother and the Area Health Authority, who had advised doctors that they could lawfully offer young people under the age of sixteen confidential advice about contraception. Victoria Gillick, a devout Catholic, objected and took the AHA to court to have its advice ruled unlawful. The highest court – the House of Lords – eventually ruled that 'parental right yields to the child's right to make his own decisions when he reaches a sufficient understanding and intelligence to be capable of making up his mind on the matter requiring decision'.

Hanging on to control
It might be assumed that this would be the end of the matter – the 'Gillick competent' child had, by this ruling, gained the legal right to make autonomous decisions, especially now this right had been further reinforced by the Children Act 1989. However, there have been a number of recent cases which have shown just how reluctant the courts still are to abandon their paternalistic role in relation to deciding on children's welfare. The recent case of **South Glamorgan C.C. v W and B** (1993) 1 FLR 574 illustrates this protectionist approach well. In this case the High Court had decided that it could not find, on the evidence presented to it, that a fifteen-year-old young woman was not of sufficient understanding to make an informed decision. Nevertheless, the High Court gave leave to the local authority (under section 100(3) of the Children Act 1989) to bring proceedings to invoke the High Court's inherent jurisdiction in the event of her refusal to submit to the medical assessment ordered under an interim Care Order (see s38(6) of the Act).

The young woman in question did indeed refuse her consent. The local authority came back and asked the court to exercise its 'inherent jurisdiction' to order that the assessment proceed, which it then did. This ruling had the effect of by-passing the 'right' explicitly given to 'mature minors' by the Children Act 1989 to refuse to submit to unwanted medical interventions.

Whatever the reasoning behind the decision, it is clear that both the local authority and the court were determined not to lose their ability to decide what they believed to be in the 'best interests' of children, irrespective of the Children Act's explicit provisions. It will remain to be seen whether this comes to be challenged or whether we will see a gradual erosion of the rights of children which have recently been accorded to them.

Fuelling adult fears

Similar fears about going 'too far' in giving children rights to self-determination can be found in the way so-called 'divorces' of children from their parents have been reported in the press. For example, in an article headlined 'Pocket money rise or it's divorce', the journalist Polly Ghazi argued:

> *Parents who turn up their noses when their children bury themselves in* Viz, Smash Hits *or* Just 17 *may be making a big mistake. The magazines may soon contain advertisements for a booklet entitled* Your Say in Court, *which could have a significant effect on family relationships. Aimed at 10- to 16-year-olds, it provides a step-by-step guide on how to 'divorce' parents.*
> (*The Observer*, 25th July, 1993)

The rest of the article is somewhat more measured in tone and explains that the booklet is produced by the Children's Legal Centre, not to incite childish rebellion but to inform children about their rights, and that it is endorsed by the NSPCC. However, the article fails to disabuse readers of the notion that children can 'divorce' their parents at will, for trivial reasons. It gives no clue about, for example, the fact that a child must seek leave of the court before being even allowed to make an application. Nor does it explain that any decision would fall far short of 'divorce', in that, even were a child to succeed in persuading the court to make an order with the effect of allowing them to live elsewhere, the child's parents would retain parental responsibility, including the right to be consulted and involved in any significant decisions about the child's upbringing (see chapter 3).

Perhaps even more disturbingly, the article makes no attempt at all to address some of the reasons why a child may seek court intervention – such as abuse or in an effort to avoid becoming a 'pawn' in parental wranglings. The message strongly presented is that allowing children access to this information – even to the magazines which advertise the booklet – is a dangerous thing to do.

This, surely, should worry us, whatever our views on the capability of children to make informed decisions. It is very disturbing that a responsible newspaper appears to be arguing for keeping children in ignorance of their legal rights. It is impossible to imagine, for example, that such a newspaper would argue to keep disabled people, refugees or convicted prisoners ignorant of their rights in law – indeed, this paper has a laudable record in exposing abuses of human rights. So what is going on?

Part of a broader movement

This is just one of many similar articles appearing in the press – one which offers a good illustration of what seems to be a much more general fear on the part of the adult world about the implications of according children certain rights. For many people the issue is simply rather too 'close to home'. Given that many of us are parents and most of us have experience of the difficulties of negotiating with children, it is distinctly uncomfortable to find out that – almost without our knowing it – legislative change is exposing our parental roles and adult authority to challenge by children. Usually the law is seen as trailing behind public opinion. Here, it would seem, the law has adopted a radical stance, with which many ordinary people feel distinctly uncomfortable.

United Nations Convention on the Rights of the Child

It is important to note that these developments in our domestic, common and statute law are not isolated events, but are, in fact, entirely consistent with moves in international law concerning children's rights. *The United Nations Convention on the Rights of the Child*, which was ratified by the UK government in December 1991, sets out a wide range of rights which children ought to enjoy. While these rights cannot be enforced in a court of law, they are a declaration of standards that the British Government has accepted and is committed to achieving.

For present purposes the following rights are the most important, in that they say something fundamental about how, in the view of the framers of the Convention, children ought to be treated in modern society:

- The right to parental care (Article 5).
- The right to family life (Article 9).
- The right to freedom of expression (Article 13).
- The right to appropriate assistance, to be given to their parents and guardians in the performance of their child-rearing responsibilities (Article 18).
- The right to protection (Article 19).

However, within the present argument, the most important right of all is that provided by Article 12, which we will therefore quote in full:

1 States parties shall assure to the child who is capable of forming his or her own views the right to express those views freely in all matters affecting the child, the views of the child being given due weight in accordance with the age and maturity of the child.
2 For this purpose, the child shall in particular be provided with the opportunity to be heard in any judicial and administrative proceedings affecting the child, either directly or through a representative or an appropriate body, in a manner consistent with the procedural rules of national law.

Of course, these different rights do not always sit easily with each other. For example, in order to protect a child it may be necessary to deprive the child of family life. In particular, it must be acknowledged that allowing children to participate in decision-making will, on occasions, expose them to risk and will reduce the ability of adults to protect them. Clearly then, putting the Convention into practice will often entail conflicts, where difficult judgements will need to be made about which one takes precedence. This is why matters of discretion are so important and why, we would argue, the child's right to be consulted is so important.

The child's voice

One of the most important innovations of the Children Act in this respect is the way it has reinforced and expanded the child's right to instruct a lawyer to act on his or her behalf. The Guardian ad Litem's role is to advise the court about the child's welfare, not to speak for the child. In acknowledging that children should also be entitled to their own legal representation, the Act is recognising, in effect, that there will be times where there is a disparity between what an adult believes is in their 'best interests' and what they, themselves, may see it to be. The lawyer is required to take instructions from the child, if the child is 'able, having regard to his understanding, to give such instructions on his own behalf' (see rule 12, Family Proceedings Courts (Children Act 1989) Rules 1991). Moreover, courts have recognised that this is a right which must not be undermined. In **Re H** (A Minor)(Care Proceedings: Child's Wishes), 1993, 1 FLR 440, where a lawyer failed to fully represent the child's viewpoint, the court held that:

> *Faced with the divergent wishes and views of the child and his Guardian ad Litem, the solicitor was in error in failing to give proper weight to the terms of r12(1)(a) and to take exclusive instructions from the child. It followed that the child had not been properly represented at the hearing ... that involved a fundamental forfeiture of the child's right.*

It would appear, then, that the law is gradually coming to recognise that children are not simply entitled to have their needs met, but have rights of self-expression and self-determination. While these are, at present, only available in some limited circumstances, we do see the law as increasingly willing to allow the child a voice.

Why we need to promote children's rights

The Children Act 1989 does not represent a fanatical and zealous children's charter, hell-bent on liberating children from the shackles of adult domination. Rather, it does no more than codify a much more universal shift – and a limited shift at that – to begin to treat children less like possessions or 'objects of concern' and more like people.

Power and control are seldom surrendered without a fight and we should, perhaps, not be surprised to see large pockets of resistance. The question is not whether inexperienced and wilful children should be given untrammelled license to do whatever takes their fancy at a particular moment – to pretend this is what is going on is to miss the point entirely. Rather, the question is how we can achieve a situation where children, given their vulnerability to adult power and their admitted inexperience, can be accorded certain basic and fundamental rights. Indeed, we would argue that the consequence of *not* giving children these rights will be to collude with their continued mistreatment.

Children are far from stupid, although, like the rest of us, they can do stupid things sometimes. If we treat them as stupid – incapable of making sensible choices, unable to ever do anything for themselves – then they will simply not tell us what they are up to or the things that worry them. They will also not ask for our help when they are in trouble, but will try to tackle their problems on their own or just decide to put up with the wrongs that are done to them – they will not forgive us for failing them. *Those* are the possibilities which should really frighten us – for they are far more risky than keeping children informed. They have, we believe, far more potential for tragedy than allowing children a limited set of legal rights.

WHAT RIGHTS SHOULD THE LAW PROMOTE?

We would argue that child welfare law, as it currently applies, has the potential to promote the following rights for children:

- The right to be taken seriously and treated with respect, irrespective of whether they are 'victims' or 'offenders' or merely 'pawns in the game'.
- The right to have their views ascertained about actions taken on their behalf and to be genuinely listened to when they express them.
- The right to be legally represented in court proceedings.
- The right to be kept informed and have actions which affect them explained to them.
- The right to be allowed access to confidential advice.
- The right to take action on their own initiative and to have some control over the processes they set in motion by doing so.
- The right to the full protection of the law if they are wronged against.
- The right to liberty, unless they are a danger to themselves or others.
- The right to a basic standard of care and to conditions which promote their life-opportunities and potentials, and which foster their healthy development.

Not all of these rights are available to children in all situations. In some respects this is because the legislative process has not been prepared to take on powerful interests. In others it is simply because children are kept in ignorance of their rights. In yet others it is because resources have not been made available. For all these shortcomings, however, we believe the law does offer a framework within which it is at least possible to promote children's rights. How much is achieved is, in the end, up to us.

Legislating adult power
Most parents, most of the time, act in their children's best interests – but some do not. All parents are also capable of sometimes allowing other considerations to cloud their judgement or to get in the way of doing what is best for their children. Parents are not saints – they get angry, they have divided loyalties, they sometimes lose their tempers and they can sometimes use their children to work out problems or ambitions of their own. Equally, professionals have their own concerns, their own battles to fight and their own needs. Once we

acknowledge that adults do not always know best and may not always act in the most honourable ways, then we need to recognise that there must be some limits on adult power. The law, in this context, is not intended to undermine an adult's ability to care about and care for children, to protect them and to promote their welfare, rather it can provide an essential counter to the *misuse* of adult power. It is this that we see as the role of law in enabling better childhoods.

Glossary

Accommodating:
one of the services that local authorities must provide for children in need. Accommodated children are not 'in care' and their parents retain full parental responsibility.

Adoption:
the total transfer of parental responsibility from the child's natural parents to the adopter(s).

Affidavit:
a statement in writing and on oath, sworn before a person who has the authority to administer it.

Appeal:
a complaint to a superior court of an 'injustice' done by an inferior one. In the context of family proceedings heard in the Magistrates' Family Proceedings Court, appeal will be to the High Court; if the proceedings are heard in the County Court or High Court, appeal will be to the Court of Appeal (see Figure 2.1).

Area Child Protection Committee (ACPC):
provides a forum for developing, monitoring and reviewing the local child protection policies, and promoting effective and harmonious co-operation between the various agencies involved (see Box 5.4).

Assessment:
a process of gathering together and evaluating information about a child, his or her family and their circumstances, in order to determine the child's needs. Its purpose is to plan for the child's immediate and long-term care and to decide what services and

resources must be provided. Detailed information about conducting assessments in child protection cases is provided in *Protecting Children: A Guide for Social Workers Undertaking a Comprehensive Assessment* (Department of Health, 1987).

Authorised person:

has two different meanings. In relation to emergency protection, care and supervision, it refers to persons, other than the local authority, who are authorised by the Secretary of State to bring proceedings. Presently this covers the NSPCC and its officers. Elsewhere in the Children Act there are references to persons who are authorised to carry out specified functions (e.g. to enter and inspect independent schools). Refer to the Act and Regulations for further information on the powers of such authorised persons.

Burden of proof:

the duty of proving one's case. The burden of proof generally lies with the plaintiff or prosecutor. It is up to the party alleging a fact that has the burden of proving that fact – this burden must be discharged by producing relevant evidence which the court accepts.

In care:

refers to a child looked after by a local authority by virtue of a Care Order under section 31(1)(a) or an interim Care Order under section 38 of the Act. The local authority has parental responsibility for the child, which it shares with the child's parents.

Child:

in law, a person under the age of eighteen. There is an important exception to this in the case of an application for financial relief by a 'child' who has reached eighteen and is, or will be, receiving education or training [Sched 1, paras 2, 6 & 16].

Child of the family:

in the context of the Children Act 1989, this phrase refers to a child of both parties to the marriage or 'any other child, not being a child who is placed with those parties as foster-parents by a local authority or voluntary organisation, who has been treated by both of those parties as a child of their family'.

Child protection conference:
a formal meeting attended by representatives from all the agencies concerned with the child's welfare. Its purpose is to gather together and evaluate all the relevant information about a child and to plan any immediate action which may be necessary to protect the child. (See Box 5.4 for details of child protection case conference).

Child Protection Register:
a central record of all children in a given area who have been identified as being at risk and for whom support is being provided via inter-agency planning (see Box 5.4).

Child-minder:
a person who looks after one or more children under the age of eight for reward for more than two hours in any one day [s71].

Children in need:
children who are entitled to services provided by a local authority, including children who are disabled [s17] (see Box 4.2).

Complaints procedure:
the procedure that the local authority must set up to hear representations regarding the provision of services under Part III of the Children Act (see Box 9.1).

Concurrent jurisdiction:
under the Children Act [s92(7)], the High Court, County Court and Magistrates' Court (Family Proceedings Court) all have jurisdiction to hear all proceedings under the Act, with some clearly limited exceptions. It is also possible for all proceedings involving the same child and family, irrespective of where they started, to be heard in the same court.

Contact:
replaces the former term 'access'. It includes visits between children and others and communication by letter and telephone.

Conviction:
when a person has been found guilty of a criminal offence.

Court welfare officer:
a probation officer appointed to provide a report for the court about the child and the child's family situation and background.

Cross-examination:
the procedure during the trial where the lawyer representing the party which did not call the witness seeks to establish its own case by questioning the other side's witness.

Day care:
a person provides day care if he or she looks after one or more children under the age of eight on non-domestic premises for more than two hours in any day [s71]. In relation to the local authority provision of day care, it refers to any form of supervised activity provided for children during the day [s18(4)].

Directions appointment:
a hearing to clarify matters in dispute, to agree evidence and to give directions as to the timetable of the case and the disclosure of evidence.

Disabled:
the Children Act defines such a child as one who 'is blind, deaf or dumb or suffers from mental disorder of any kind or is substantially and permanently handicapped by illness, injury or congenital deformity or such other disability as may be prescribed' [s17(11)].

Discharge:
an application to terminate an earlier order. In relation to an Emergency Protection Order (EPO), while there can be no appeal against the making or refusal to make an EPO, there can be an application to discharge the EPO after 72 hours.

Disclosure interview:
a term sometimes used to indicate an interview with a child, conducted as part of the assessment for suspected sexual abuse. It is misleading (since it implies, in some people's view, undue pressure on the child to 'disclose') and therefore the preferred term is 'investigative interview'.

Duty to investigate:
the local authority's statutory duty to investigate a child's circumstances in order to see whether action needs to be taken to safeguard the child's welfare [s47(1)].

Education welfare officers (EWOs):
provide social work support to children in the context of their education, including seeking to ensure that children receive adequate and appropriate education, and that any special needs are met. They also provide more general liaison between local authority education and social services departments.

Educational psychologists:
conduct evaluations of children's educational, psychological and emotional needs, offer therapy and contribute psychological expertise to the process of assessment.

Evidence-in-chief:
the evidence which a witness gives in response to examination on behalf of the party who has called the person as a witness.

Evidence:
consists of the testimony (oral evidence) of witnesses, documents (e.g. a welfare report) and objects provided to a court in support of a case. (See Box 5.3 for information about evidence in criminal proceedings).

Ex parte:
in law this refers to having heard one side only. For instance an *ex parte* injunction is an injunction granted after having heard only one party. It is of an emergency character.

Family centre:
a centre which the child, parents and any other person looking after the child can attend for occupational and recreational activities, advice, guidance or counselling, and accommodation while receiving such advice, guidance or counselling [Sched 2, para 9].

Family panel:
the new panel from which the magistrates who sit in the new Family Proceedings Court are selected.

Family Proceedings Court:

the new court at the level of the Magistrates' Court to hear proceedings under the Children Act 1989.

Family proceedings:

any proceedings under the inherent jurisdiction of the High Court in relation to children and under Parts I, II and IV of the Children Act 1989, the Matrimonial Causes Act 1973, the Domestic Violence and Matrimonial Proceedings Act 1976, the Adoption Act 1976, the Domestic Proceedings and Magistrates' Courts Act 1978, sections 1 and 9 of the Matrimonial Homes Act 1983 and Part III of the Matrimonial and Family Proceedings Act 1984. Proceedings under Part V of the Children Act 1989 (i.e. orders for the protection of children) are *not* family proceedings.

Fieldworkers (field social workers):

conduct a range of social work functions in the community and in other settings (e.g. hospitals). Most fieldworkers carry their own case-load and, following career progression, undertake supervision of others and/or specialise either with a particular group (e.g. older people) or in a particular function (e.g. running the home-help service). In many (but by no means all) local authorities, specialist social workers have been appointed to co-ordinate child protection work and offer particular expertise (e.g. in conducting joint investigative interviews with police officers).

Foster carers:

provide medium- and long-term substitute family care for children. Short-term care of children under eight may be subject to the child-minding provisions in Part X.

Guardians ad Litem (GALs):

officers of the court appointed to investigate a child's circumstances and to report to the court. The GAL does not represent the child but seeks to present a non-partisan view of the child's welfare. The GAL can appoint a solicitor to represent the child. In some cases the Official Solicitor acts as the GAL.

Guidance:

issued by the Secretary of State setting out how legislation is to be applied in 'good practice'. Although it does not have the full force of law, it may be quoted or used in court proceedings.

Harm:
defined in the Children Act as 'ill-treatment or the impairment of health or development', where 'health' refers to physical or mental health and 'ill-treatment' is taken to include sexual abuse and forms of ill-treatment which are not physical [s31(9)].

Hearsay:
second-hand information (which the witness did not see or hear for him or herself), which a witness, while giving evidence in court, recounts to prove what he or she is saying is true. Generally, hearsay evidence is not allowed in criminal proceedings, whereas in child welfare cases in civil courts this rule over hearsay has been relaxed. Words and conduct (e.g. nodding one's head) are only hearsay if used to 'prove' their truth.

Independent visitor:
appointed by a local authority for a child in care who has the duty of 'visiting, advising and befriending the child' [Sched 2, para 17].

Inherent jurisdiction:
the powers of the High Court to make orders to protect a child which are not based on statute.

Injunction:
an order made by the court prohibiting an act or requiring its cessation. Injunctions can be either interlocutory (i.e. temporary, pending the outcome of the full hearing) or perpetual.

Inter-agency plan:
a plan devised jointly by the agencies concerned in a child's welfare, which co-ordinates the services they provide (see Box 5.4).

Investigative interview:
the preferred term for an interview conducted with a child as part of an assessment, following concerns that the child may have been abused (most notably in cases of suspected sexual abuse). It

is usually conducted jointly by specially trained social workers and police officers. The Home Office *Memorandum of Good Practice* may be followed.

Judicial review:

where a decision made by a public body or official is challenged in the High Court.

Keyworker:

a social worker allocated specific responsibility for a particular child. In residential settings, this will be the person who will maintain an overall interest in the child's welfare and will often undertake specific work with the child on a day-to-day basis. In a fieldwork child care setting, the keyworker is appointed at a child protection case conference and is responsible for co-ordinating the work done with and for the child by the different agencies (see Box 5.4).

Leading question:

a question which either suggests the required answer (e.g. 'Daddy hurt you, didn't he?') or which is based on an assumption of facts not yet established (e.g. 'When did you first tell anyone about what Mummy did?', when the child has not yet stated that Mummy did anything).

Legal aid:

available in proceedings under the Act. There is neither a merits nor a means test in relation to special Children Act proceedings relating to Secure Accommodation, Care, Supervision, Child Assessment and Emergency Protection Orders, and in relation to any child in the proceedings.

Looked after:

a child is looked after when he or she is in local authority care or is being provided with accommodation by the local authority [s22(1)].

Memorandum of Good Practice:

published by the Home Office in conjunction with the Department of Health in 1992 to assist those making a video recording of an interview with a child witness, where it is intended that the recording should be acceptable in criminal proceedings.

Monitoring:

where plans for a child, and the child's safety and wellbeing, are systematically appraised on a routine basis. Its function is to oversee the child's continued welfare and to enable any necessary action or change to be instigated speedily and at a managerial level, to ensure that proper professional standards are being maintained.

Notice:

the minimum period of time (this varies according to the order being sought and the circumstances of the application), prior to the hearing or a directions appointment, that respondents and others entitled to notice must be given.

Official Solicitor:

an officer of the Supreme Court who acts on behalf of children in certain cases. When representing a child, the Official Solicitor acts both as a solicitor as well as a Guardian ad Litem.

Paramountcy principle:

the principle that the welfare of the child is the paramount consideration in proceedings concerning children.

Parental responsibility:

defined as 'all the rights, duties, powers, responsibilities and authority which, by law, a parent of a child has in relation to the child and his property' [s3(1)] (see Box 3.1).

Parties:

parties to proceedings are entitled to attend the hearing, present their case and examine witnesses. Children are automatically parties in section 31 proceedings and in proceedings under Part V.

Permanency planning:

deciding on the long-term future of children who have been moved from their families. Its purpose is to ensure them a permanent, stable and secure upbringing, either within their original family or by providing high-quality alternative parenting or care.

Police protection:

section 46 allows the police to detain a child or prevent his or her removal for up to 72 hours, if they believe that the child would otherwise suffer significant harm.

Probation officers:

employed as officers of the court and financed jointly by the local authority and the Home Office. In addition to taking on a case-load, most probation officers undertake some specialist work, such as conducting group-work with offenders or helping to run a phone-in service.

Refuge:

a 'safe house' operating under a certificate issued by the Secretary of State, providing asylum for children who have run away from home or local authority care [s51].

Regulations:

supplementary powers issued by the Secretary of State under the authority of an Act, which have the full force of law.

Rehabilitation:

in a child care context, this is the process of working with children and parents and providing resources and support to enable children to return home to be brought up in their families. It involves meeting the children's needs and helping to overcome the problems that led to their needing to live away.

Representations:

see complaints procedure.

Residential social workers:

provide day-to-day care, support and therapy for children living in residential settings, such as children's homes.

Respite care:

a service giving family members or other carers short breaks from their caring responsibilities. It is intended to support the care of people (e.g. those with disabilities or infirmities) in the community who might otherwise need to be placed in full-time residential care.

Respondent:

the party required to reply to an application or an appeal.

Responsible person:

This has two meanings in the Children Act. First, in relation to a supervised child, the responsible person is 'any person who has parental responsibility for the child, and any other person with whom the child is living'. With their consent the responsible person can be required to comply with certain directions [Sched 3, paras 1 & 3]. Second, in relation to a Recovery Order, the responsible person means any person who has the care of the child by virtue of a Care Order or an Emergency Protection Order, or who has the child in police protection.

Reviews:

regular meetings held by local authorities to monitor the progress of children they are looking after, providing opportunities to consider progress, any problems and changes in circumstances, and to resolve difficulties, set new goals and plan for the future.

Rules of Court:

lay down the procedural rules which govern the operation of the courts. They have the full force of law.

Section 8 orders:

the four new orders contained in the Children Act for resolving disputes about children's upbringing: Contact, Residence, Specific Issue and Prohibited Steps Orders.

Secure accommodation:

placing children and young people in accommodation which restricts their liberty, to prevent them harming themselves or others (see Box 9.2).

Social workers:

a generic term applying to a wide range of staff who undertake different kinds of social welfare responsibilities. These include advising and supporting individuals and families during periods of trouble, both within the community and in residential settings; accessing resources, benefits and services; conducting assessments and investigations, and monitoring standards of care. Social workers may be employed by local authorities or voluntary organisations (see residential social worker, fieldworker, education welfare officer and probation officer).

Standard of Proof:
the basis on which a case must be proved. In civil proceedings it is generally on a 'balance of probabilities', but in criminal proceedings it is 'beyond reasonable doubt'.

Statement of Arrangements for Children:
a detailed statement of arrangements for the child considered by the judge in divorce proceedings. If, having considered the statement of arrangements, the judge is satisfied that the court need not exercise its powers under the Children Act 1989, the judge will certify accordingly. If the judge is not satisfied, he or she can direct that further evidence be filed, order a welfare report or require one of the parties to attend the court.

Supervisor:
the person under whose supervision the child is placed by virtue of an order under sections 31 and 38. The powers and duties of the supervisor are contained in section 35 and Schedule 3.

Timetables:
under the Children Act the court, in fulfilling its obligation to avoid delay [s1(2)], has the power to draw up a timetable and give directions for the conduct of the case in any proceedings in which the making of a section 8 order arises, and in applications for Care and Supervision Orders [ss11 & 32].

Transitional arrangements:
the arrangements relating to children who are the subjects of existing orders under legislation prior to the implementation of the Children Act 1989. The general rule is that where this is the case, the child will be treated as if he or she were the subject of the nearest equivalent order in the Act.

Variation:
an application to vary an order seeks an adjustment of the terms of the order.

Vexatious litigant:
an applicant who makes repeat applications for court orders, seen as doing so in order to harass or disturb the other party.

Ward of court:
a child who, as the subject of wardship proceedings, is under the protection of the High Court. No important decision can be taken regarding the child while he or she is a ward of court, without the consent of the wardship court.

Wardship:
the legal process whereby control is exercised over the child in order to protect the child and safeguard his or her welfare.

Welfare checklist:
refers to the checklist contained in section 1(3) of the Act (see Box 2.1.)

Welfare report:
section 7 of the Children Act gives the court the power to request a report on any question in respect of a child under the Act. The report can be presented by either a probation officer or an officer of the local authority. The court may take account of any statement contained in the report and any evidence given in respect of matters referred to in the report, as long as the court considers them relevant.

Written agreement:
an agreement arrived at between the local authority and the parents of children for whom it is providing services. It is not a legal contract. These agreements are part of the partnership model that is seen as good practice under the Act.

Further reading and useful addresses

FURTHER READING

In this book we have avoided referencing in the text, to make it more 'user-friendly'. For those readers who wish to know more or to have access to information for reference, we have set out some suggestions here.

Government publications

There are four main documents to which all those working with children and young people should at least have access – better still if you can get your own copies, for reading and for reference:

Department of Health (1989) *An Introduction to the Children Act*. HMSO: London.
Department of Health (1990) *The Care of Children: Principles and Practice in Regulations and Guidance*. HMSO: London.
Department of Health, Department of Education and Science and the Welsh Office (1991) *Working Together under the Children Act 1989: A Guide to the Arrangements for Inter-agency Co-operation for the Protection of Children from Abuse*. HMSO: London.
Department of Health (1987) *Protecting Children: A Guide for Social Workers Undertaking a Comprehensive Assessment* HMSO: London.

Regulations and Guidance
In addition you should equip yourself with the appropriate volume(s) of *Guidance and Regulations* which apply to your area of work.

Department of Health (1991) *The Children Act 1989: Guidance and Regulations, Volume 1, Court Orders.* HMSO: London.

Department of Health (1991) *The Children Act 1989: Guidance and Regulations, Volume 2, Family Support, Day Care and Educational Provision for Young Children.* HMSO: London.

Department of Health (1991) *The Children Act 1989: Guidance and Regulations, Volume 3, Family Placements.* HMSO: London.

Department of Health (1991) *The Children Act 1989: Guidance and Regulations, Volume 4, Residential Care.* HMSO: London.

Department of Health (1991) *The Children Act 1989: Guidance and Regulations, Volume 5, Independent Schools.* HMSO: London.

Department of Health (1991) *The Children Act 1989: Guidance and Regulations, Volume 6, Children with Disabilities.* HMSO: London.

Department of Health (1991) *The Children Act 1989: Guidance and Regulations, Volume 7, Guardians ad Litem and Other Court Related Issues.* HMSO: London.

Department of Health (1991) *The Children Act 1989: Guidance and Regulations, Volume 8, Private Fostering and Miscellaneous.* HMSO: London.

Department of Health (1991) *The Children Act 1989: Guidance and Regulations, Volume 9, Adoption Issues.* HMSO: London.

Department of Health (1993) *Guidance on Permissable Forms of Control.* Department of Health

Department of the Environment (1991) *Code of Guidance for Local Authorities on Homelessness.* HMSO: London.

General books on the Children Act 1989

Probably the best general text which contains a full copy of the Children Act 1989 is:

Masson, J. and Morris, M. (1992) *Children Act Manual.* Sweet & Maxwell: London.

This is fairly 'lawyerly', but does give a section-by-section annotation on the Act's provisions. Other readable general texts include:

Allen, N. (1992) *Making Sense of the Children Act* (2nd Edition). Longman: Harlow, Essex.

Bainham, A. (1990) *Children, The New Law: The Children Act 1989*. Jordan: Bristol.

Freeman, M. D. A. (1992) *Children, Their Families and the Law: Working with the Children Act*. Macmillan: Basingstoke.

We suggest you get at least one of these, if you need a more comprehensive knowledge of the Act and its detailed provisions. A more speculative text, which seeks to contextualise the Act and raise issues about children's rights in particular, is:

Eekelaar, J. and Dingwall, R. (1990) *The Reform of Child Care Law: A Practical Guide to the Children Act 1989*. Routledge: London.

The law

Probably the best and most readable general text which explains the basic processes and principles of law, and which has some coverage of the Children Act is:

Brayne, H. and Martin, G. (1990) *Law for Social Workers*. Blackstone: London.

The following text is of a more scholarly nature, exploring not just the legislation but how it was formulated:

Parton, N. (1991) *Governing the Family: Child Care, Child Protection and the State*. Macmillan: Basingstoke.

A critique of the law in its relationship to child welfare is provided by:

King, M. and Trowell, J. (1992) *Children's Welfare and the Law: The Limits of Legal Intervention*. Sage: London.

The following is of use in respect to legal aspects of co-habiting parents:

Priest, J. (1993) *Families Outside Marriage* (2nd Edition). Family Law/Jordan: Bristol.

This booklet is about the impact of domestic violence upon children and the legal remedies:

Legal Action Group (1993) *Family Emergency Procedures*. Legal
Action Group: London.

Education

The Department of Education commissioned a special booklet to
provide a guide to the Children Act 1989 for those working in
the education sector:

The Open University (1991) *The Children Act 1989: A Guide for
the Education Service*. The Open University: Milton Keynes.

The Association of Teachers and Lecturers has also produced a
booklet which is clear and easy to read and offers practical
advice, for example, about teachers appearing as witnesses and
strategies for avoiding allegations of abuse:

Sage, G. (1993) *Child Abuse and the Children Act: A Critical
Analysis of the Teacher's Role*. Association of Teachers and
Lecturers: London.

The following is of particular interest to those working with
children with special educational needs:

Chasty, H. and Friel. J. (1993) *Caught in the Act: Children with
Special Needs; Assessment, Law and Practice*. Jessica Kingsley:
London.

This book makes special reference to child protection in an
education setting:

Brock, E. (1992) *Child Abuse and the Schools' Response: A
Workshop for Professionals Involved with Children and
Young People for Nursery to Further Education*. Longmans:
London.

Health

The Department of Health has produced a training pack for
health professionals, to help them gain knowledge and
understanding of how the Children Act 1989 applies to their
work. It can be used for individual or group learning:

Department of Health (1992) *The Children Act 1989: NHS Study and Training Pack*. HMSO: London.

There are also a number of other Government documents designed for particular groups and purposes.

Department of Health (1992) *The Children Act 1989: An Introductory Guide for the NHS*. Health Publications Unit: Heywood, Lancashire.

Department of Health (1988) *Diagnosis of Child Sexual Abuse: Guidance for Doctors: Standing Medical Advisory Committee Report*. HMSO: London.

Department of Health (1991) *The Welfare of Children and Young People in Hospital*. HMSO: London.

Department of Health (1992) *The Children Act 1989: What Every Nurse, Health Visitor and Midwife Needs to Know*. HMSO: London.

Department of Health (1992) *Child Protection: Guidance for Senior Nurses, Health Visitors and Midwives: Standing Nursing and Midwifery Advisory Committtee Report*. HMSO: London.

Department of Health (1992) *Children and HIV. Guidance for Local Authorities*. Department of Health: Manchester.

National Health Service Management Executive (1990) *A Guide to Consent for Examination and Treatment*. NHSME.

National Health Service Management Executive (1991) *Access to Health Records Act 1990: A Guide for the NHS*. NHSME.

Books and other publications of particular interest to health professionals are:

Mitchell, B. and Prince, A. (1992) *The Children Act and Medical Practice*. Family Law/Jordan: Bristol.

Royal College of Surgeons (1991) *Physical Signs of Sexual Abuse in Children*. Royal College of Surgeons: London.

Slater, M. (1993) *Health for All our Children: Achieving Appropriate Health Care for Black and Ethnic Minority Children and their Families*. Action for Sick Children: London.

Cloke, C. and Naish, J. (1992) *Key Issues in Child Protection for Health Visitors and Nurses*. Longman: London.

Child protection

There are vast numbers of books on this topic – we have chosen just a few that we ourselves find useful. Of particular interest to practitioners are:

Adcock, M., White, R. and Hollows, A. (1991) *Significant Harm: Its Management and Outcome*. Significant Publications: Croydon.

Cooper, D. (1993) *Child Abuse Revisited: Children, Society and Social Work*. Open University Press: Buckingham.

Corby, B. (1993) *Child Abuse: Towards a Knowledge Base*. Open University Press: Buckingham.

Hallett, C. and Birchall, E. (1992) *Co-ordination and Child Protection: A Review of the Literature*. HMSO: London.

Inglis, R. (1978) *Sins of the Fathers: A Study of the Physcial and Emotional Abuse of Children*. Owen: London.

Wattam, C. (1993) *Making a Case in Child Protection*. Longman: London.

Two books offer specific critiques of mistakes:

Howitt, D. (1992) *Child Abuse Errors: Social and Psychological Explanations*. Harvester Wheatsheaf: Hemel Hempstead.

Reder, P., Duncan, S. and Gray, M. (1993) *Beyond Blame: Child Abuse Tragedies Revisited*. Routledge: London.

These two books both contain a series of chapters, written by different authors, which take a more theoretical and analytical approach.

Stainton Rogers, W., Hevey, D., Roche, J. and Ash, E. (eds) (1992) *Child Abuse and Neglect: Facing the Challenge* (2nd Edition). Batsford: London.

The Violence Against Children Study Group (1990) *Taking Child Abuse Seriously: Contemporary Issues in Child Protection Theory and Practice*. Unwin Hyman: London.

For those who wish to follow up the various inquiries that have been conducted into cases of child abuse, there is a review:

Department of Health (1991) *Child Abuse: A Study of Inquiry Reports 1980–1989*. HMSO: London.

Probably the most instructive recent inquiry reports which offer detailed analysis of the problems and specific advice for improvement are:

Blom-Cooper, L. (1985) *A Child in Trust. The Report of the Panel of Inquiry into the Circumstances Surrounding the Death of Jasmine Beckford*. London Borough of Brent: London.

Butler-Sloss, E. (1989) *Report of the Inquiry into Child Abuse in Cleveland*. HMSO: London (Cd.412).

Clyde, W. (1992) *Report of the Inquiry into the Removal of Children from Orkney in February 1991*. Scottish Office: Edinburgh.

Kirkwood, A. (1993) *The Leicestershire Inquiry 1992: The Report of the Inquiry into Aspects of the Management of Children's Homes in Leicestershire Between 1973 and 1986*. Leicestershire County Council: Leicestershire.

Levy, A. and Kahan, B. (1990) *The Pindown Experience and the Protection of Children: The Report of the Staffordshire Child Care Inquiry*. Staffordshire County Council: Staffordshire.

Child witnessess

Anybody directly involved in interviewing children will need to consult:

Home Office in conjunction with Department of Health (1992) *Memorandum of Good Practice: Video Recorded Interviews with Child Witnesses for Criminal Proceedings*. Home Office: London.

The Department of Health commissioned a training pack, to be used in respect to investigative interviewing with children:

Open University (1993) *Investigative Interviewing with Children*. Open University: Milton Keynes.

The following was written especially for child witnesses, to help them prepare for court:

NSPCC (1993) *Child Witness Pack*. NSPCC: London.

General books and articles useful in this field are:

Flin, R. and Boon, J. (1989) 'The child witness in court' in *Child Sexual Abuse: Listening, Hearing and Validating the Experiences of Children*, Wattam, C. *et al.* (eds). Longman: London.

Jones, D.P.H. (1992) *Interviewing the Sexually Abused Child: Investigation of Suspected Abuse* (4th Edition). Gaskell/Royal College of Psychiatrists.

Spencer J.R. and Flin, R. (1990) *The Evidence of Children: The Law and the Psychology*. Blackstone: London.

Stone, M. (1984) *Proof of Fact in Criminal Trials*. W. Green and Son: Edinburgh.

Stone, M. (1988) *Cross-examination in Criminal Trials*, Butterworths: London.

Walker, P. N. and Wrightsman, L.S. (1991) *The Child Witness: Legal Issues and Dilemmas*. Sage: London.

Wells, J. (1989) 'Powerplays – considerations in communicating with children' in *Child Sexual Abuse: Listening, Hearing and Validating the Experiences of Children*, Wattam, C. *et al.* (eds). Longman: London.

Residential care

Department of Health (1993) *Residential Care for Children: A Review of the Research*. HMSO: London.

Harris, R. and Timms, N. (1993) *Secure Accommodation in Child Care: Between Hospital and Prison or Thereabouts?* Routledge: London.

Utting, W. (1991) *Children in the Public Care: A Review of Residential Care*. HMSO: London.

Children's rights

General books in this field include:

Alston, P., Parker, S. and Seymour, J. (eds) (1992) *Children, Rights and the Law*. Clarendon: Oxford.

Flekkoy, M. F. (1991) *A Voice for Children*. Jessica Kingsley: London.

Freeman, M. D. A. (1983) *The Rights and Wrongs of Children*. Frances Pinter: London.

Newell, P. (1989) *Children are People Too: The Case Against Physical Punishment*. Bedford Square: London.

Newell, P. (1991) *The UN Convention and Children's Rights in the UK*. National Children's Bureau: London.

Stainton Rogers, R. and Stainton Rogers, W. (1992) *Stories of Childhood: Shifting Agendas of Child Concern*. Harvester Wheatsheaf: Hemel Hempstead.

Booklets setting out children's rights include:

Children's Legal Centre (1993) *Your Say in Court*. Children's Legal Centre: London.

Alone in London Service Advocacy Project (1993) *Hitting Home: A Guide to the Children Act for Homeless Young People*. CHAR: London.

National Council of Voluntary Child Care Organisations (1993) *Checklist for Developing Complaints Procedures in Voluntary Child Care Organisations*. NCVCCO: London.

The UN Convention on the Rights of the Child is available from the Children's Rights Development Unit (see overleaf).

USEFUL ADDRESSES

Association of Lawyers for Children, Griffiths Robertson, 46 West Street, Reading, Berks RG1 1TZ. Telephone: 0734 574018.

Association of Teachers and Lecturers, 7 Northumberland Street, London WC2N 5DA.

The Centre for the Study of Law, The Child and the Family, Department of Law, Brunel University, Uxbridge, Middlesex UB8 3PH. Telephone 0895 274000.

CHAR, 5–15 Cromer Street, London WC1H 8LS. Telephone: 071 833 2071.

Childline, 50 Studd Street, London N1 0QJ. Telephone: 071 239 1060.

Children's Legal Centre, 20 Compton Terrace, London N1 2UN. Telephone: 071 359 9392.

Children's Rights Development Unit, 235 Shaftesbury Avenue, London, WC2H 8EL. Telephone: 071 240 4449.

Family Rights Group, The Print House, 18 Ashwin Street, London E8 3DL. Telephone 071 923 2628.

Health Publications Unit, No. 2 Site, Heywood Stores, Manchester Road, Heywood, Lancashire DL10 2PZ.

Legal Action Group, 242 Pentonville Road, London N1 9UN. Telephone: 071 833 2931.

National Association of Young People in Care (NAYPIC), 20 Compton Terrace, London N1 2VN. Telephone: 071 226 7102 or 23 New Mount Street, Manchester M4 4DE. Telephone: 061 953 4501.

National Children's Bureau, 8 Wakley Street, London EC1V 7QE. Telephone: 071 278 9441.

NCVCCO, Unit 4, Pride Court, White Lion Street, London N1 9PF. Telephone: 071 833 3319.

NSPCC, 42 Curtain Road, London EC2A 3NH. Telephone: 071 825 2500.

Open University, School of Health, Welfare and Community Education, Walton Hall, Milton Keynes MK7 6AA. Telephone: 0908 653743.

The Registrar General, The General Register Office, Adoptions Section, Smedley Hydro, Trafalgar Road, Birkdale, Southport PR8 2HH.

REUNITE (National Campaign for Abducted Children),PO BOX 4, London WC1X 8XY. Telephone: 071 404 8356.

Voice for the Child in Care, Interchange Studios, 15 Wilkin Street, London NW5 3NG.

Index

For ease of use, this index is not exhaustive. It indicates the main sections where a term is defined or a topic is discussed. Equally, only legislation other than the 1989 Children Act is included, given that the Children Act is so pervasive throughout the book. Locating particular aspects of the Children Act can also be done via the list of boxes on pages iv–v.